Cultural Revolution and Industrial Organization in China

Cultural Revolution and Industrial Organization in China

Changes in Management and the Division of Labor

by Charles Bettelheim

Translated by Alfred Ehrenfeld

Monthly Review Press
New York and London

Library of Congress Cataloging in Publication Data
Bettelheim, Charles.
    Cultural revolution and industrial organization in
China.
    Translation of Révolution culturelle et organisation
industrielle en Chine.
    1. Industrial management—China. 2. Textile indus-
try and fabrics—China—Management. 3. Employees'
representation in management—China. I. Title.
HD70.C5B4813   658.4'00951   73-90078
ISBN O-85345-314-4

First Modern Reader Paperback Edition 1975

15   14   13   12   11   10   9   8   4   6   5   4

Monthly Review Press
62 West 14th Street, New York, N.Y. 10011
47 Red Lion Street, London WC1R 4PF

Manufactured in the United States of America

Contents

Preface

This book does not propose to describe the numerous and manifold changes that have occurred, and still are occurring, in that vast country which is China. It would be senseless for a foreign visitor to attempt such a task. The intended purpose, rather, is to arrive at some theoretical conclusions regarding the implications of the changes the Cultural Revolution has effected in the factories of China. The transformations to be discussed were described to me during my visits to a number of factories in 1971. Their impact has been substantiated by numerous articles published in China, which merit the closest attention, both in terms of the facts they describe and in terms of their political orientation.

The book relies heavily on material I gathered during my stay in China in August and September 1971. Two women students (who wish to remain anonymous) planned and edited a portion of it, using notes taken during my seminar report at the Ecole Pratique des Hautes Etudes, material I brought back with me, and the text of a lecture I delivered in Paris in November 1971. The book is also based on observations made during earlier trips, in 1958, 1964, and 1967, and on the published and oral accounts by numerous foreign visitors—workers, peasants, economists, sociologists, etc.— who have visited China recently.

The book deals largely with changes as they have affected industrial management and the division of labor in industry. I regard these changes as extremely important. Although the transformations in question were given an unprecedented impulse by the Cultural Revolution, it should not be concluded that they originated with this revolution or were the only ones to occur in recent years.

Several points must be stressed. First, the changes in question gained their present impact only because of the defeat of Liu Shao-chi's bourgeois political line.[1] The adherents of this line had in effect begun to challenge similar changes initiated in 1958 during the Great Leap Forward. On the other hand, these transformations correspond to an ideological revolution marking the beginning of an upheaval in manners and customs which is increasingly giving rise to a new proletarian morality.[2]

Furthermore, the massive changes that occurred in the Chinese countryside after the formation of people's communes in 1958 continued and were strengthened during the Cultural Revolution. Between 1960 and 1966, the adherents of Liu Shao-chi's line had tried to undermine the economic and social changes initiated in the countryside during the Great Leap Forward. The Cultural Revolution that followed was to provide the impetus for a massive socialist counter-offensive, especially in the area of rural industrialization, which has already substantially transformed Chinese village life. Here, too, the Cultural Revolution posed a challenge to the immemorial division of labor and, notably, to the division between town and countryside, that underlies the divisions between social classes.

1. Communist parties characterize as "bourgeois" a political line which objectively opposes viable changes that would reduce the influence of capitalist or bourgeois factors in the economic base or in the superstructure. The predominance of such a line leads to the consolidation (an outcome that can be prevented) of capitalist forms of the division of labor and of industrial management, as well as of bourgeois positions in general. The bourgeoisie consists not only of former capitalists, landowners, etc., but also of cadres, technicians, and administrators who use their positions to undermine the workers' collective control over the employment of the means of production and the direction of investments.

2. See my article in *Le Monde diplomatique*, November 1971.

The Great Proletarian Cultural Revolution thus represents an ideological and political struggle the effects of which bear both on the economic base and on the superstructure, destroying the old social relationships and giving rise to new ones. The very fluctuations of the struggle which unfolded during the Great Proletarian Cultural Revolution evidence the degree to which its outcome depended both on the mass movement and on its correct orientation by a revolutionary leadership.

At each stage of the Cultural Revolution, the adherents of Mao Tse-tung's revolutionary line had to accomplish an enormous labor of discussion. At the outset, for instance, it took several months for the workers to rebel against the prevailing methods of management and the division of labor and against the diehard supporters of the existing relations in the factories. It was only gradually, through the give and take of prolonged discussion, that they began to realize that the old relations were obstructing progress along the road to socialism. When I visited China in 1967 the members of various revolutionary factory committees told me that during its initial stages they believed the Cultural Revolution to be concerned only with literature and the arts, and that they had distrusted the critics of the situation in their own factories. Eventually they came to understand that the prevailing conditions in the factories had to be changed before further advances along the road to socialism could be made.

Later, when confronted with the task of elaborating new relations, the workers were often at odds about how to interpret the slogans of the revolutionary line. Months and even years of discussion and struggle were required to achieve the unity indispensable to the success of the Cultural Revolution.[3] Through discussions and struggles involving millions of workers and vast sections of the population, a

3. Concerning the initial stages of the Cultural Revolution, see the important book by Jean Daubier, *Histoire de la révolution culturelle prolétarienne en Chine* (Paris: Maspero, 1970). My postscript to this book deals with the question of the "ultra-left" and with the significance of its intervention.

new road was opened up in the struggle for socialism. There is no precedent for such an attempt to transform social relations. It constitutes a decisive and permanent achievement, as decisive and permanent as any scientific or social experiment which discovers new processes or new objective laws.

In brief, this book argues that the Great Proletarian Cultural Revolution represents a turning point of the greatest political importance; it "discovered" (in the sense in which Marx used the expression in connection with the Paris Commune) an essential form of the class struggle for the construction of socialism. It will be recalled that Marx stressed the significance of the Paris Commune in these words: "The struggle of the working class . . . has entered upon a new phase with the struggle in Paris. Whatever the immediate results may be, a new point of departure of world-historic importance has been gained."[4]

Part 1 discusses the essential features of the changes that have occurred both in the management of industrial enterprises and in the division of labor within these enterprises. It is largely an account of my conversations with the members of the revolutionary committee at the General Knitwear Factory in Peking. This factory was the scene of a vast social transformation, and the changes it witnessed have occurred, in varying degrees, in all the factories I visited, as well as in those discussed both in the Chinese press and in the reports of the visitors mentioned earlier. These changes are in keeping with the primary thrust of the Cultural Revolution, which became the focus of the struggle waged by the adherents of the revolutionary line, and continues to be supported by the Chinese Communist Party through its measures, slogans, and directives.

Part 2 is a relatively brief outline of the guiding political principles of Chinese planning. Although these principles were operative before the Cultural Revolution, their appli-

4. Karl Marx, *Letter to Kugelmann*, April 17, 1871.

cation was then frequently frustrated by the "centralizing" tendency abetted by Liu Shao-chi's line. The new impetus given to the implementation of these principles is designed, within an indispensable coordinating framework, to allow local and provincial authorities the broadest possible initiative, and to enable the workers to take a substantial part in decision making during the planning stage.

Part 3 discusses the significance, principles, and perspectives of the main thrust of the Chinese Revolution—the gradual elimination of the distinction between performance tasks and administrative tasks, between manual labor and intellectual labor, and between town and countryside. This is the road outlined by Marx and Engels.

Part 4 discusses the political principles that were implemented during the Cultural Revolution, and advances some theoretical conclusions regarding the revolutionizing of the social relations of production.

—Paris, January 1973

1. The General Knitwear Factory

Organization and Policies

The General Knitwear Factory in Peking was built in 1952 and is located in the center of the city. In 1971 it employed 3,400 people, 60 percent of whom were women. Production is diversified and ranges from weaving (cotton and synthetic fabrics) to finished goods (sweaters, jackets, etc.). Total annual output is on the order of 20 million items. The factory produces for the domestic market as well as for export to Southeast Asia, the Middle East, Africa, and Eastern Europe.

The three principal shops are devoted to weaving, bleaching, and sewing. There are also auxiliary shops, including a shop for general mechanical work, where machinery is repaired or modified. The factory includes a child-care center where children can be boarded for as long as a week, and a canteen which serves three meals a day. Two women workers and the vice-chairman of the revolutionary committee gave the following account of the workers' living and working conditions in this factory:

"We pay particular attention to working conditions and are guided in this by the Chinese Communist Party. We are concerned with the welfare of the workers and the preservation of human initiative. In the old society things were very different. The capitalists did not care about such matters.

"The shops have air conditioners that maintain an even temperature. Elaborate safeguards protect the workers against injury from their machines. These protective devices are occasionally disregarded and a few accidents have occurred, but they are very rare. A few installations are not safe and must be replaced. Some shops, such as the one containing the dryers, are excessively hot; the workers in that area receive a special allowance, eat more meat, and rest more frequently. What matters, however, is to reduce the heat. A high temperature around the dryers is inevitable, but every effort is made to minimize its effects on the surrounding areas. You have seen wagons that carry ice; this is one of the ways in which we try to reduce the heat. Bathing facilities are also available to the workers.

"In the sewing shops we work eight hours a day and take half an hour for a meal. There are two additional fifteen-minute breaks for physical exercises designed to prevent work-related disabilities. These are at the same time military exercises, for we must all be prepared in case of an imperialist invasion.

"Our factory has an infirmary, and in every shop there are barefoot doctors.[1] All doctors attached to the infirmary are required to make daily rounds of the shops. This reduces the need for a worker to consult a doctor elsewhere. If sick workers cannot be properly treated in the factory, they are immediately sent to a hospital. A hospital is located right across from the factory, and there is another one in this district. There is no charge for consultation and medication. The workers get their regular pay while out sick.

1. In addition to the doctors trained in medical schools, China has over a million doctors who received rapid training (often after an initial practice such as nursing). These "barefoot doctors" continue to participate in production while devoting a portion of their time to preventive medicine and ordinary medical care. The term "barefoot doctors" derives from the fact that in southern China, where rice constitutes the chief crop, the peasants customarily work barefoot in the rice fields. When barefoot doctors cannot easily handle cases, they direct the patient to a specialized center where more skilled treatment is available. This is an example of the manner in which the Chinese masses themselves deal with the solution of their problems.

"Of course, we do not claim that we have done enough to improve working conditions. We must make even greater efforts, for there are always new problems to be solved. The world changes all the time and new contradictions keep cropping up.

"Women get an extra day off each month. Those who are seven months pregnant work seven hours per day instead of eight. When their work is particularly difficult, as in the case of pedal-operated sewing machines, pregnant women do this work only during the first six months of pregnancy, and are then given different jobs. In case of special difficulties, the doctor may recommend a change of work. After a normal confinement, a woman receives a fifty-six-day paid maternity leave. In case of a more difficult confinement, this leave is increased to seventy days. Until her child is one year old, a breast-feeding mother gets two additional thirty-minute breaks a day to nurse her baby; this is reduced to a single thirty-minute period a day during the next six months. Breast feeding is discontinued when the child reaches the age of eighteen months. Between the ages of eighteen months and seven years, children remain full time in the nursery, and stay with their families only once a week; but mothers who do not want to leave them there full time may leave them in the nursery for the afternoon or for the day. In any case, there is enough room for all the children. We don't know the exact number of babies between the ages of fifty-six days and three years. The children between the ages of three years and seven years—those who have not reached school age—number slightly over two hundred.

"Factory pay averages 54 yuan per month, ranging from a high of 102 to a low of 30. Minimum living expenses per person and per month come to about 12 yuan. In cases where all the members of the factory worker's family do not earn 12 yuan, an allowance is provided. Retired workers receive 60 percent of their pay."

Following are some average wages in other factories. In

Peking, the pay in 1972 of workers in the petrochemical industry, in Knitwear Factory No. 2, and in construction, averaged 60 yuan, ranging from 35 to 40 yuan to 90 to 102 yuan, depending on the factory. At the textile factory, the engineers, technicians, and cadres earned about 150 yuan.

In Shenyang, wages at the heavy machinery factory averaged 65 yuan, ranging from 35 to 114 yuan. At the transformer factory, wages in 1971 averaged 63 yuan, ranging from 33 to 104 yuan. Technicians at this factory started at 32 yuan if they were middle school graduates, at 46 yuan if they received a higher education. Three out of 453 technicians earned 225 yuan (these were old technicians who were allowed the pay they used to get). The average pay of 61 yuan for technicians was due to the fact that they included many young people.

In Shanghai, at Plastic Materials Factory No. 3, pay averaged 65 yuan, ranging from 40 to 100 yuan. Technicians earned between 50 and 110 yuan, apprentices between 18 and 23 yuan, depending on seniority.

In the district factories, average wages were slightly lower. In one district of Kuantung, the wages of workers in two factories averaged 45 yuan, ranging from 32.5 to 100 yuan.

The more important factories have various kinds of schools where workers can acquire new knowledge and prepare for new responsibilities. The courses vary in length with the material taught. It takes two years, for instance, for an experienced worker to become an engineer. The Chinese are struggling to replace the notion of "professional advancement" with that of "serving the people"—being useful to the collectivity. This idea is basic in China, and implies a profound ideological transformation. As will be seen, it permeates the mass organizations, party committees, etc., as well as the relations between factories, planning, and so on. Today, new political responsibilities do not entail a change in wages. Wage ranges are still under discussion. The problem cannot be solved quickly, for extensive investigation is required to determine the nature of a proper wage policy at the present time. Once this policy has been determined, a great deal of discussion and persuasion is required so as to avoid imposing decisions on those who are not "enemies of the people."

The vice-chairman of the factory revolutionary committee explained current policies at the factory. He stressed the slogan "politics in command" and contrasted it with the attitudes prevailing before the Cultural Revolution.

"Chairman Mao has said that in industry we must follow the example of Taching and implement the Anshan Constitution. Implementing the Anshan Constitution means always to put politics in command, strengthen party leadership, launch vigorous mass movements, systematically promote the participation of cadres in productive labor and of workers in management, reform any unreasonable rules, assure close cooperation among workers, cadres [in China, "cadres" refers to political cadres], and technicians, and energetically promote the technical revolution. These are the basic ideas of the Anshan Constitution. Before the Cultural Revolution we rarely put politics in command."

The case of Taching is a concrete example of how the notion of "politics in command" transforms the relations of production. Taching is a petroleum complex which began operations in 1960 after Soviet supplies were halted, an event which necessitated the most rapid expansion and utilization of Chinese resources. In view of China's lack of drilling equipment, this required an exceptional effort on the part of the workers. The Taching workers did not work in order to earn incentive bonuses, but to serve the people and the revolution. This involved a mass struggle. The petroleum technicians were not merely administrators but were integrated into the work brigades. All problems were discussed daily and collectively; it was thus possible to arrive at solutions transcending a narrow technical outlook. New methods of extraction were put into practice. The result has been that China now holds the world record in terms of international drilling norms.

Annual production of crude oil continues to increase by about 30 percent. In terms of its oil requirements, China is now self-sufficient. Taching represents for Chinese industry what Tachai represents for agriculture. It points to the socialist road of industrialization.

The vice-chairman of the revolutionary committee went on to explain that formerly in the factory economics was in command, which meant priority of production, a system of material incentives (bonuses), relying on specialists and experts to run the factory, priority of technique, money, and profit. The "two participations" approach—participation by political cadres in production and by workers in management—although well known in principle ever since the Anshan Constitution (1960), existed only in theory. It was the Cultural Revolution which propagated it among the workers, who then increasingly demanded its general application. Today the workers see to it that the cadres participate actively in production work; the cadres and technicians, for their part, regard such participation as correct and indispensable.

"Before the Cultural Revolution I was assistant director of this factory; in this capacity I implemented the revisionist line. I did not understand what was meant by putting proletarian politics in command, nor did I understand that there were two headquarters within the party. I concentrated on production and technology. I demanded that the workers devote themselves to production—production, production, always production. When the workers failed to fulfill the plan, they were offered material incentives, bonuses. In the old days there were twenty-eight different kinds of bonuses— monthly, quarterly, annual bonuses for those who exceeded the established norms, bonuses for quality work. . . . There were also bonuses for those who devoted themselves entirely to their work, without thinking of anything else, without thinking of moving elsewhere. We had some workers from Shanghai who were always thinking of their native province.

To keep them quiet and tied to their jobs, we gave them bonuses."

Before the Cultural Revolution, moreover, there was a division between workers and management. The chief criterion of achievement was technical expertise, which meant that workers could not pass judgment on the activities of management. The factory manager was appointed by the central administration. He had considerable powers and could make unilateral decisions, but he had very little contact with the workers. Some party cadres shared this unquestioning belief in technical expertise, and this weakened the bonds between the workers and the Chinese Communist Party. The factory party committee made no effort to build the party and strengthen its leadership role. It concerned itself, in fact, only with production. The workers used to call the former secretary of the party committee "secretary of production."

"Before the great upsurge of the Cultural Revolution I did not understand what was meant by 'cultural revolution.' I thought it had to do only with cultural circles and education. The more we defended interests opposed to those of the masses, the more the masses criticized us by means of *tatzupao* [handwritten wall posters], which they hung on the walls."

The factory used to be run in keeping with an essentially revisionist line which stressed production, bonuses, the importance of experts and technique. In this factory as well as in others, this line made it possible for the enemies of socialism to assume leading positions. These elements were eliminated by the Cultural Revolution—through the intervention of the workers guided by the central leadership of the Chinese Communist Party. In June 1969, during the Cultural Revolution, the factory party committee was dissolved and replaced with a new committee. Generally speaking, the Cultural Revolution has profoundly transformed the structure and operation of the factories.

The General Knitwear Factory affords a concrete instance

of this general transformation. Its history during the Cultural Revolution provides us with the basic features of these changes. In the production units, the Cultural Revolution pursued the objectives of correcting the role and work of the cadres, strengthening the relations between cadres and workers, changing the style of management, and promoting a socialist outlook in everyday life—a proletarian morality based on a proletarian world outlook (in family life, production, etc.). Central to this vision is the will to subordinate individual and particular interests to the overall interests of the revolution.

Substantial progress was made toward the realization of these objectives when the masses began to appropriate revolutionary ideas. This involves a study of the basic writings of Marx, Lenin, and Mao Tse-tung while relating this study to practice. It also requires collective discussion and study, both inside and outside the factory (in the family, for instance). These collective discussions take many forms. Their primary focus is the effort to understand Marxism and to struggle against revisionism and its ideological consequences.

One aspect of this activity was the mass movement of criticism directed against the errors of the factory cadres. Its aim was not to eliminate these cadres, except when they had made serious errors, but to help them learn from their mistakes and assimilate revolutionary ideas and the revolutionary line. Wherever the old cadres were reinstated, this was done by the masses. Many of them, after having been criticized, would have preferred not to resume their functions—largely because, under the influence of the "ultra-leftist" line, criticism was extended to cadres who had committed only slight errors, and sometimes assumed brutal forms (including physical assault). Such methods, instead of helping the cadres correct their practice in keeping with the directives of the party Central Committee, tended to demoralize them and induce them to limit themselves to work involving little political responsibility (see Postscript). It was emphasized that this criticism was meant not to punish, but to educate as many people as possible.

This movement of criticism brought about profound changes both in ideas and in the everyday relationships between workers and cadres, and was made possible by the unifying role of the Chinese Communist Party. Party intervention was of a general character; it influenced the workers even in cases when—as happened in this factory—the *local* party organizations were temporarily shaken up.

Mass Organizations in the Production Units

The Cultural Revolution saw the emergence of new mass organizations which, aided and guided by the Central Committee, were gradually modified and unified. At the General Knitwear Factory in 1971 these organizations consisted of the workers' management teams, the Red Guards, and the revolutionary committees, all of which came into existence following the dissolution of the factory party committee. Similar organizations, not always bearing the same names, have been formed or are being formed in many other Chinese factories. The General Knitwear Factory is a model factory in terms of the new management relations.

The Workers' Management Teams

Li Chou-hsia, a woman worker and member of the Peking factory's revolutionary committee, described the workers' management teams and their functions. During the Cultural Revolution, she explained, the masses not only rejected the revisionist line, but were also strengthened in struggle; steeped in the study and application of Mao Tse-tung Thought, they demanded participation in management, in keeping with the Anshan Constitution.

The first experiment in workers' participation in management was sponsored by the revolutionary committee before the formation of the new party committee. Initiated in a single shop, it was extended throughout the factory in February 1969. The experiment focused on the abolition of the "unreasonable rules" imposed by the old management—regulations concerning work organization, discipline, etc., which reflected a lack of confidence in workers' initiative and thus tended to preserve capitalist relations. Each regulation was subjected to mass discussion. Although this process is still going on, a great number of rules have already been abolished, making it possible to effect a substantial reduction in factory administrative personnel.

The formation of workers' management teams and their function of acting as a control on the cadres provoked a real class struggle. The very principle underlying the formation of these teams had been opposed from the first, both by members of the old management staff and by a number of workers. The most common objection consisted in the assertion that the factory already had or soon would have a party committee, party cells, a revolutionary committee, and that workers' management teams were therefore superfluous. A member of the revolutionary committee stressed the fact that these arguments were immediately taken over by class enemies:

"These class enemies realized that the formation of workers' management teams would result in the presence of hundreds of activists. They understood that their subversive activities would be closely scrutinized by large numbers of workers. It is clear, therefore, that these teams emerged, expanded, and were strengthened in the context of the struggle between two roads, two classes, and two lines."

The election of workers' management teams is organized by the members of a work team or shop and is entirely under their supervision; management is concerned only with the principle of workers' management teams. Team members are elected at various levels corresponding to the levels at which the teams themselves are organized—factory, shops, work teams. This gives them a solid representative base among the workers. Candidates must be actively engaged in the study and application of Marxism-Leninism and Mao Tse-tung Thought, have some experience, and be representative of the masses.

The General Textile Factory of Peking has an election once a year; former members may be reelected if they enjoy the confidence of the workers. The election is organized by the workers themselves, who draw up a list of candidates after extensive discussion. The teams consist of veteran workers, who play the leading role, former cadres who have rejoined the rank and file, and young intellectuals. Team members are all production workers; they receive no extra pay and work at least one additional hour a day in connection with their functions (attending meetings, visiting workers' homes, etc.).

The workers' management teams focus on orientation, inspection, investigation, ideological work, and correct style of work, rather than on management as such, which is the responsibility of the revolutionary committee.[2] Both the workers' management teams and the revolutionary committee are under the ideological and political direction of the party committee.

The teams have five areas of concern: (1) ideological and political work; (2) production work and technical revolution; (3) financial and material matters (cost control, investments, etc.); (4) work safety; and (5) general welfare. They function as intermediaries between management and the masses and act as a control on the managerial bodies, as well as on the party members and administrative departments. Political problems are placed in the forefront.

2. The teams therefore have nothing in common with the Yugoslav practice of self-management. Their aim is not to ensure profitability and maximize profit but to serve the interests of the people.

Li Chou-hsia explained it as follows:

"Now that these teams exist, the emphasis is no longer only on mutual aid and comradeship but also on helping party members. In the old days a party member was regarded only as a moving force and not as a possible target of the revolution as well. In fact, there are living ideas among the masses, and it is necessary to organize discussions with the party members so that they may benefit ideologically from contact with the workers. The comrades used to be reluctant to help party members, but the workers' management teams have changed this situation. The masses now take the initiative in going to the party members to further the ideological revolutionization of the party."

This ideological revolutionizing activity among party members—due to the initiative of the masses and to intervention by the workers' management teams—is of decisive importance. It aims at a radical transformation of practice and ideas by ridding them of bourgeois ideological influences. It helps shatter the myth that party members are custodians of Marxism-Leninism and proletarian ideology, who stand above the masses and may criticize them while remaining exempt from their criticism.

The Cultural Revolution has helped shatter this myth. In principle, only cadres and functionaries may be subjected to public criticism. The ideological revolutionization of ordinary workers is pursued primarily through the collective study of Marxism-Leninism, and in private and family discussions. Ideological revolutionizing activity is therefore no longer the political concern of the cadres alone. As a member of the revolutionary committee put it, "Today everybody is involved in political work." The extension of this political activity is making it increasingly difficult for cadres to place themselves above the workers, and is steadily reducing the possibilities for the growth of capitalist tendencies.

The workers' management teams are called on to assist management: to make suggestions in all five areas of their concern, discuss them in the shops and among the work teams, stimulate workers' initiative and coordinate their ideas, aid the revolutionary committee, and formulate criticism. They act as intermediaries between management and workers, encouraging the workers to discuss the proposals and decisions of management, and informing management of the workers' opinions. They thus establish links "from the top down and from the base up." Criticism from the rank and file is considered the most important. It helps management correct its style of work, and makes it possible to check on the cadres, their decisions, and the manner in which these are implemented. All these activities are inspired by collective expressions of opinion.

The workers' management teams are also concerned with relations between the workers of their own factory and those of other factories. There are numerous contacts between the teams of various production units. At the General Knitwear Factory, the teams deal with problems involving the upgrading of product quality. There is no department of quality control. The system is one of self-control and each work team controls its own work. The workers make every effort to find collective solutions to whatever problems come up.

The workers' management teams are also involved in planning factory output. The workers are repeatedly consulted before a plan is formally adopted. The planning project is scrutinized concretely in terms of how it will affect each shop and each work team. The workers divide into small groups for this purpose, which enables them to express themselves fully on the plan's significance, its implications for each worker, and on possible improvements in terms of production, quality, product diversification, etc. This results in numerous exchanges between workers and managerial bodies, with the workers' management teams acting as go-betweens. The overall plan is thus scrutinized repeatedly, and its final adoption is the outcome of a common effort by the various work teams and shops. The same method of multiple exchanges "from the top down and from the base up" has been adopted between the factories and various specialized agencies (see Chapter 2).

Working closely with the workers and the three-in-one teams (cadres, technicians, workers), the workers' management teams make a thorough review of possible innovations and modifications that could help reduce investment costs. In the General Knitwear Factory, as well as in many other Chinese factories, investment estimates initially projected for the plan are frequently lowered following examination by the workshops concerned and by the general machine shop. (Almost all Chinese factories have a shop for general mechanical work which plays a very important role. It repairs and modifies materials, and achieves innovations within the factory itself. In rural districts, the general machine shop is always among the first to be established; it keeps in constant touch with local factories.)

The notion of "relying on one's own strength" has a profound effect on the attitude toward the requirements of accumulation. "In keeping with Chairman Mao's teachings," a member of the revolutionary committee explained, "a three-in-one team has been organized in our factory for the purpose of achieving a technical revolution. This is a specialized team, but a campaign is under way to enlist mass participation in this effort. We must not rely exclusively on this specialized team which, at any rate, consists of few people.

"The objectives of this technical revolution are suggested by the various shops and are designed to upgrade quality, increase productivity, ensure safe working conditions, and reduce work tensions. These are generally the areas in which technical innovations are achieved. This approach may result in the development of new raw materials, new techniques, new technologies, new installations, and new methods.

"Certain changes enable us also to improve quality and make labor less burdensome. In the dyeing and printing shop, for instance, everything used to be done by hand. This shop is being upgraded, but we still lack a number of machines. Those you saw this morning, which can dye and print an entire roll of jersey, were made with the help of old machines we received from another factory. The experts and specialists had always claimed that this type of machine could not possibly dye and print jersey in two colors. The workers said: 'Why can't it be done? Let's try it!' After the Cultural Revolution, they proposed the attempt be made, and after a few trials it turned out to be quite practical to print in two colors. Nevertheless, we still have problems.

"The sewing shop has machines that make it possible to cut out sleeves and sew them onto jackets in a single operation. Each machine requires but one operator, and this new technique represents progress. But the work is very hard—the worker must simultaneously hold the cloth with her hands and operate the foot pedals, and give her full attention to this job eight hours a day. Some women workers said that this improved technique is not really an improvement because the women who operate these machines get no rest at all. A few of these machines were set aside, and we studied the problem with the operators. We succeeded in modifying the machines by eliminating the pedals.

"There were other problems. It was necessary, for instance, to cut the threads between the pieces to separate them. Here too we solved the problem through innovation— the pieces are now made and overlapped automatically, and the worker has only to position the cloth and hold it in place by hand. If this machine were in general use, the length of apprenticeship—six months in the case of the old foot-operated machines—and labor intensity could be considerably reduced.

"We are always looking for new improvements and new ways to reduce waste. These technical innovations are an important means of developing industry. Our approach requires big machines which we will develop in due time. It is well worth taking two or even five years to develop a good machine. What matters most is for the workers themselves to take the initiative in determining the need for innovation, for the working class must liberate itself."

Both in the General Knitwear Factory and in numerous other Chinese factories, the innovations achieved through mass initiative are sometimes of a high technical order. They are often created locally, but a Chinese factory is not a closed world and innovations are widely circulated among factories under the impetus of the workers' management teams.

The teams report their activities at meetings and discussions attended by all the workers of the shop or by all work teams concerned, listen to criticism, and see to it that the workers' ideas are given full consideration. The procedure is the same as that followed in the elaboration of the plan. When there are too many workers in a shop for discussion purposes, they break up into small groups where they can all express their opinions. A member of the revolutionary committee stressed the fact that no decision is made at any level without prior consultation with the workers. He added: "If the leading cadres were permitted to make their own decisions, even the new cadres might eventually follow the old road."

Members of the workers' management teams attend the meetings of the party committee cells at the appropriate level—work team, shop, factory. (The party also holds separate meetings at which its particular problems are discussed.) These meetings are held in the factory. The workers' management teams have their own meetings: once a month on the factory level, every two weeks on the shop level, every day on the work team level. The daily meetings deal with problems that come up during the day, and a balance sheet is drawn up every evening. The problems may touch on relations with the cadres, on political questions, or on everyday life (housing, relocation, personal and family matters, etc.). Factory or shop managers do not attend these meetings, which furthers workers' initiative and prevents the workers' management teams from getting caught up in an administrative web.

The workers' management teams organize the study of the basic works of Marx, Lenin, and Mao Tse-tung. In their role of acting as a control and stimulating initiative, they help the party committee and the revolutionary committee resolve political and ideological questions. Since these committees are mass groupings, they must follow the leadership of the party, which plays a decisive role in determining their ideological orientation. Problems that arise between the party and the workers' management teams are settled through discussion—party leadership is *political*, not administrative. The leadership of the party committee or cell is exercised jointly with the workers' management teams in common meetings where those affected by the decisions can participate in the discussions; decisions made without full consultation with the masses may well be inadequate. Decisions made at the shop or work team levels, however, are not transmitted by the workers' management team representatives but by the party cell secretaries or by the representatives of the administrative management team in each shop.

"The extension of workers' management team activity," explained Comrade Lie, "entails several advantages: it enables the workers to give full expression to their initiative, apply their intelligence and wisdom, gain experience in collective management of a socialist enterprise, and develop lower-echelon cadres. Vice-chairman Lin Piao has said that ours are mass policies, democratic policies. Management, therefore, is not the exclusive concern of a handful of people, but must involve everyone. The activities of the workers' management teams accurately reflect the need to implement this slogan. Everybody is involved in political and ideological work."[3]

3. When I visited this factory, great progress had already been made in the struggle against the "ultra-left" (see Postscript) but it was not generally known that this faction was headed by highly placed officials such as Lin Piao. It should be noted, however, that this mention of Lin Piao's name was quite exceptional in my experience.

When this study was made during the summer of 1971, the workers' management teams were still in the process of formation. As Comrade Lie explained: "We are still in a trial stage. Our activities are inspired by the Anshan Constitution. Their orientation is correct. As for concrete methods, we shall see . . ."

The role played by the workers' management teams at the General Knitwear Factory may be assumed, in other factories, by similar organizations bearing a different name. These are sometimes under the direction of the workers' representative conference, elected by the workers of the factory. This body plays manifestly the same role as the old labor unions. These frequently disappeared from the scene during the Cultural Revolution because they did not truly speak for the masses but constituted bureaucratic bodies whose leading members had become integrated into management which they had ceased to criticize. Accordingly, instead of going to the roots of workers' discontent whenever it manifested itself, and thus helping the revolution, the labor union functionaries merely tried to cool tempers or abate the dissatisfaction by splitting the working class. Before the Cultural Revolution "bureaucratization" had infected most of the mass organizations—of youth, women, etc.—and their activities have since been almost entirely suspended, at least nationally. The problem of restructuring these organizations and redefining the conditions under which they can resume functioning under the effective control of the masses is currently the subject of widespread discussion.

Unlike the former labor union leaders, the members of the workers' management teams or of the conference standing committees are full-time production workers. They are thus much less likely to isolate themselves from the workers or side with factory management should it follow the revisionist road.

These comments are not meant to imply that the formation of workers' management teams or of workers' representative conferences constitutes an "absolute guarantee" against "economism" and revisionism, or against a general orientation contrary to the requirements of socialist construction. The various formations may themselves succumb to the influence of bourgeois ideology and hence become incapable of furthering the process of ideological revolutionization. This is precisely why these groupings, as well as the other mass organizations, must be placed under the ideological and political direction of the dictatorship of the proletariat and of its instrument, the Communist Party. Since it can never be guaranteed that workers' management teams or other mass organizations will retain their revolutionary ideological character, the question of their ideological revolutionization is constantly on the agenda.

This is how the matter is dealt with at the General Knitwear Factory. The following points are most strongly emphasized: the need for members of the workers' management teams to further their personal ideological revolutionization through the study and application of Marxism-Leninism and Mao Tse-tung Thought; the need for team members to remain production workers and be constantly subject to criticism by the masses; and, above all, the need for the teams to be under the *ideological leadership* of the party committee, which is itself controlled by the workers. The need for the masses to exercise permanent control is one of the points most frequently stressed.

"Within the workers' management teams, there are regular style-of-work rectification campaigns, either at the factory level or at the shop level. Workers will always have criticisms—working people always have plenty to say. To correct errors rapidly, it is necessary to launch vigorous and regular campaigns designed to rectify style of work. Workers sometimes express severe criticism. When their criticism is justified, it is accepted. Criticism that is not altogether justified is listened to patiently; and even when it has no foundation, the fact that it was made is considered encouraging."

This means, in effect, that the masses do not hesitate to express their opinions when they are convinced that the members being criticized can be induced to mend their ways. The workers' management teams thus constitute one of the organizational forms enabling the workers, through an effective practice, to appropriate Marxism-Leninism and Mao Tse-tung Thought, and hence to act as a control on the cadres and leaders, in keeping with the requirements of socialist construction.

The Red Guards

The Red Guards are not exactly a mass organization; they represent a form of individual participation in management activities. At the General Knitwear Factory, this organization began to function at the end of 1968, before the workers' management teams.[4]

Red Guards are elected individually—there is no election slate. The workers discuss each candidate, giving full consideration to his or her ideological level.

"A comrade who lags behind ideologically cannot become a Red Guard. One of the essential functions of the Red Guards is to disseminate the thought of Chairman Mao and to grasp the living ideas of the masses. How could they help others in this respect if they lag behind ideologically?"

The Red Guards do not constitute permanent groups that hold regular meetings. In fact, they do not constitute a "group"; their responsibility toward the workers is a personal one. Their ideological and political work is all the more extensive since they are more numerous than the members of the workers' management teams. The latter must always have

4. Information obtained during study trips made in 1972 appears to indicate that the kind of "individual" participation represented by the Red Guards was a transitory form which is being increasingly replaced with collective forms. This comment affords an opportunity to emphasize once again the "experimental," and hence dynamic and diversified, character of the organizational forms under discussion.

been elected Red Guards, whereas the contrary is not necessarily the case.

The activities of the Red Guards and of the workers' management teams are closely related. The Red Guards in effect act as a control on the teams: they record the workers' criticisms and opinions regarding the effectiveness of the workers' management teams, the revolutionary committee, and the party committee. This activity is designed to prevent these groupings from isolating themselves from the masses. The Red Guards thus further the ideological revolutionization of the factory, help the leadership of each work team organize study groups, and play an important role in analyzing the ideas of the masses and refuting revisionist ideas on the spot.

In view of the very considerable role played by the workers' management teams and the Red Guards in furthering ideological revolutionization, it may be useful to give some concrete examples of their activities at the General Knitwear Factory.

The first example concerns a young shop delegate who had gradually become preoccupied with production to the exclusion of all other concerns. The workers were displeased with his attitude, and reproved him for no longer putting politics in command. The various work teams in his shop met to discuss the matter and decided to criticize him. Using the public address system, a member of the workers' management team then proceeded to detail the criticisms the work teams had voiced in their discussions. The delegate's initial reaction was to reject the criticism—he felt ashamed and resented the fact that he had been criticized publicly.

"The workers explained to him that there had been private discussions, but that he had turned a deaf ear and that it had therefore become necessary to raise the matter publicly. The members of the Red Guards and the workers' management team then reviewed the entire problem with him. Proceeding from the slogan 'make the revolution and promote production,' they undertook a painstaking and patient effort to raise his level of political consciousness and induce him to accept the criticism and transform himself."

The second example involves the secretary of a shop party cell. The workers' management team considered this cadre's attitude incorrect. Before confronting him the team consulted with the shop workers and together they reviewed his attitude. The discussion resulted in a picturesque statement which reproached the cadre for having four faces: (1) smiling when being praised; (2) ashamed when being criticized; (3) displeased when confronting difficulties; and (4) a face turned away from the masses. This composite description was accompanied by a list of some one hundred specific criticisms.

The cadre was at first quite upset and did not grasp the significance of the criticism. Finally—these discussions may go on for days—he said that he was being rebuked for his character, which he had "inherited from his mother," and for which he was not responsible. The workers then "explained that what was involved was not his character but his world outlook, which had to be changed," that he had to accept the need for a discussion of how his style of work could be corrected, and that he should not think that he was incapable of changing. Each criticism was discussed in detail, and the cadre gradually corrected his relationship to the masses. The workers then took his measure once again: "His four faces have been transformed into four struggles: faced with praise, he struggles against pride; faced with criticism, he struggles against displeasure; faced with difficulties, he struggles against discouragement; and when his style of leadership isolates him from the masses, he struggles against his bureaucratic tendencies."

The workers may also criticize the cadres through *tatzupao,* through direct or indirect attacks on a functionary, or by citing quotations that are forwarded by a delegation. Criticism is always organized; it never flows from individual initiative, but results from collective decisions generally based on an overall estimate of the cadre in question. Criticism focuses on specific points which are examined in the light of the basic principles of Marxism-Leninism. Cadres may be criticized publicly, but this is not always the case; the masses decide collectively whether or not it is necessary. Workers, on the other hand, are not supposed to be criticized publicly, but in private discussions involving members of their families. This procedure avoids placing workers in unpleasant situations and confronting them in the presence of their fellow workers.

The Revolutionary Committee

The revolutionary committee is an administrative body under the political leadership of the factory party committee, and is in charge of the implementation of established policy. The revolutionary committees emerged in a number of factories during the struggles against revisionist management, at a time when the factory party committees were paralyzed. Initially they were supposed to be provisional organs, but their provisional character was rarely alluded to in the years that followed. It appears that it is being recalled more frequently of late. The vice-chairman of the revolutionary committee explained its work:

"Sometimes we get caught up in administrative detail and neglect political and ideological work. When our revolutionary committee began to function, for instance, we made a tremendous fuss and spent all our time trying to run everything by telephone. The masses told us that this wouldn't do. During the ensuing discussion, the representatives of the masses told me that ideological work has to come first. This was a good lesson. From then on, I changed my style of work and paid more attention to the overall situation in the factory."

The revolutionary committee is in charge of relations between factories, and between the factory and the planning agencies. It supervises the implementation of the plan, which is drawn up according to overall political decisions, as will be seen in Part 2. The Cultural Revolution has abolished the post of factory director. Management functions are now assumed by the chairman and vice-chairman of the revolutionary committee; the chairman is accountable to the higher departments. Final commitments with respect to the plan or other factories (e.g., delivery dates) are the responsibility of the chairman of the revolutionary committee, but these decisions are made only after consultation with the workers. This is an example of what the Chinese call "multiple initiative, individual responsibility."

The revolutionary committee is an elected body; its numerical composition is decided by the workers themselves. They draw up a slate which forms the basis for extensive discussion during which the number of candidates is narrowed down. The factory workers then proceed to a final vote. In the factories I visited, the revolutionary committees consist largely of production workers who retain their regular jobs and pay.

The revolutionary committee at the General Knitwear Factory has twenty-one members. It is based on a three-in-one combination of representatives of the masses, cadres, and soldiers of the People's Liberation Army, as well as on a three-in-one age-group combination of young, middle-aged, and older members. The twenty-one committee members include only two women. This under-representation of women is a remnant of the past, and as one of the committee members commented: "We'll have to deal with this at the next election, for as Chairman Mao has said: "Women hold up half the sky.' "

The revolutionary committee also passes on the hiring of new workers, although workers move to another factory very infrequently, for a factory is more than a production unit, it is a center of collective living. Contrary to practice in the

U.S.S.R., work books, or obligatory personal employment records, do not exist in China. The revolutionary committee and the two administrative bodies that work closely with it—the production team and the ideological and political work team—submit a quarterly report to the workers' management teams. This report analyzes the problems and difficulties encountered during the preceding period. It is scrutinized by the workers' management teams, who then formulate their criticisms and suggestions after consultation with the workers.

The Party Committee

In accordance with the decisions of the Ninth Congress of the Chinese Communist Party, new factory party committees were established during the Cultural Revolution. The General Knitwear Factory provides a typical example of how the new party committees came into existence.

There was no factory party committee between 1966 and 1969. The emphasis during this period was on ridding the party of cadres taking the capitalist road, and creating conditions conducive to the self-transformation of the old committee members. The masses were enlisted in a vast movement to purify the party ranks. This project was accompanied by a "revolutionary campaign to promote the creative study of Chairman Mao's works," which in turn led to the emergence of a revolutionary cadre.

The purification effort was intended to achieve a clear demarcation between genuine party members and those who were in fact disguised enemies. To this end the workers widely debated and criticized the leaders' practices, mistakes, world outlooks, etc. This process continued throughout the Cultural Revolution. It initially included the participation of various mass groupings which, while claiming to abide by Mao's thought, actually followed a different line.

A crucial stage in this process was that of the "Great

Alliance"—the attempt to unify the various mass organizations. The effort failed in a number of factories, and members of the People's Liberation Army (PLA) intervened to give political assistance to the workers. The Great Alliance eventually came into being. The next stage was that of the three-in-one combination—the creation of a revolutionary core acting as a provisional organ of power and consisting of representatives of the mass organizations, cadres "looked after" by the masses, and members of the PLA.

The nationwide party purification effort was carried out under the direction of the Chinese Communist Party, which defined correct practice, while *Hongqi (Red Flag),* the theoretical monthly of the Central Committee, published concrete examples and general directives. It was based largely on a general appraisal of the overall situation and on investigations by the workers. These investigations were designed to evaluate the prior practices of each party member and were frequently conducted in the rural areas or factories where the cadres in question had previously lived or worked.[5]

Subjecting the party cadres to mass criticism modified their relations with the workers. The election of the new committee thus took place in the context of a party which had been purified in every area of production. In preparation for the election, the masses were asked to determine the numerical composition of the committee (this varied in each factory) and to establish a list of candidates. At the General Knitwear Factory, the list included some forty names, with twenty-seven to be elected.

The workers engaged in a thoroughgoing debate to designate the twenty-seven individuals considered most competent to constitute the party committee. These discussions, and the task of coordinating the workers' views of the candidates, were organized by the revolutionary core of the three-in-one

5. As will be seen in the Postscript, the "ultra-left" frequently turned similar investigations into instruments of personal struggle, thus seriously undermining the ideological struggle.

combination. The process has been described as consisting successively of a democratic discussion, a concentration (a meeting to establish consensus), and renewed discussion with the masses. In all it consisted of "four discussions and three concentrations." The last concentration was followed by a meeting of the entire party membership and by the election of the party committee officials. Only party members could vote in this election.

The election list is conceived not only in terms of personalities, but is also based on certain criteria: the committee must include representatives of different parts of the factory, all the shop cell secretaries, and delegates from the workers— a point not widely observed before the Cultural Revolution— and it must adhere to the principle of the three-in-one age-group combination. At the General Knitwear Factory, the party committee has also been confronted with the woman question. The need for the participation of women in the party committee has not received sufficient attention. The committee includes only five women, although women represent 60 percent of the factory workers. The matter was the subject of self-criticism, and the party committee is to be changed accordingly. This question has been dealt with in general resolutions of the Central Committee.

The leadership and management structure of the General Knitwear Factory, which is similar to that found in most factories, may be summarized as follows:

The party committee constitutes the political leadership of the factory, and is supported by a revolutionary committee and workers' management teams. The revolutionary committee has a tripartite composition; the workers' management teams consist only of workers. In addition to the party committee, which exercises overall leadership, the party has cells at the shop and work team levels. In every factory the revolutionary committee implements the revolutionary line as defined by the party committee. Factory management, which is the responsibility of the revolutionary committee, can thus be viewed as a particular instance of the implementation of the political line.

There is frequently some overlap between the responsibilities of the party committee and those of the revolutionary committee. The findings of a partial investigation carried out in Shanghai factories, for instance, indicate that 70 percent of party committee members are also members of revolutionary committees, and that 49 percent of revolutionary committee members are party members. At the General Knitwear Factory, the leading members of the party committee are also the leading members of the revolutionary committee—the vice-chairman of the revolutionary committee is also vice-secretary of the party committee, and the secretary of the party committee is also chairman of the revolutionary committee.

The workers' management teams assist the party committee and the revolutionary committee. They act as intermediaries between the masses and the leadership and management bodies. They also act as a control on the activities of the party committee, the revolutionary committee, the administrative agencies, and the party cadres.

Generally speaking, the Cultural Revolution has effected significant changes in the composition of the Chinese Communist Party throughout the country. An investigation of the scope of these changes had not yet been completed in the summer of 1971. The findings of a partial investigation of 1,119 factories in the municipality of Shanghai, however, provide some indications in this respect. The municipality of Shanghai constitutes an urban and rural complex of about 10.7 million people, of whom 5.8 million live in the urban center. Following the consolidation of the party, former leaders constituted only 37 percent of the 4,532 leading members of the factory party committees. (Consolidation differs from purification in that it entails changes in responsibilities and not their abolition.) Most of the new party committee members are party cadres of relatively long standing.

The Chinese stress the fact that there were very few workers in the party committees before the Cultural Revolution. The majority of the new cadres have come out of the mass movement that emerged during the Cultural Revolution, or are former rank and filers.

The renovation of the party committees does not mean that those who were dismissed were considered bad elements; most of them occupy other posts today, and their removal from the party committees was influenced by the need to renovate the committees and assimilate young cadres. Young members represent 10 percent of the party committees in the factories surveyed. The expression "young members" designates both those under thirty and new members of any age.

There were very few expulsions on the party committee level; in the 1,119 factories surveyed, only 1.2 percent of former members were repudiated. Legal sanctions are not applied in this context—cadres who have made serious mistakes are dismissed; those who are merely incompetent and have not made serious mistakes are asked to withdraw from the party. Cadres who did not make serious mistakes but were regarded as unfit for their task by the masses may at their own request engage in a process of reeducation, either by rejoining the base, or by attending a "May 7th school." The May 7th schools are new production units established by the cadres. There appears to be no hierarchy in these schools. They are set up by the first arrivals, who build everything from scratch. The cadres work very hard. The first arrivals must construct housing, work the land, dig wells. They often lack the necessary experience and seek advice from the peasants in the neighboring people's communes. As the school gets organized, workshops and even small factories may be added. The day is spent in productive labor (usually in the morning), and in the study and discussion of Marxism-Leninism and Mao Tse-tung's works. The May 7th schools foster an ideological revolutionization which is particularly important for cadres, such as administrative employees, who are not ordinarily involved in production.

Reeducation of cadres through manual labor was practiced before the Cultural Revolution, but the May 7th schools have added a new dimension: in addition to manual labor, the course involves intensive ideological work. Both kinds of activity are carried out in close conjunction.

Reeducation is regarded as an honor. The period of reeducation is of unspecified duration. Attendance at a May 7th school is not obligatory but must be requested by a cadre. All cadres, even those who have made no mistakes, may request attendance at these schools provided their committee considers their absence justified and unlikely to interfere with production. The masses are also consulted about the application. Cadres must obtain the consent of the factory and district party committees and of the May 7th school workers and revolutionary committee. The course may last from six months to one or two years. Cadres may be asked to leave the school whenever they are needed elsewhere.

The organs of power have undergone changes the depth of which is not adequately conveyed in statistical terms. A far from insignificant number of their members of long standing have been subjected to mass criticism, and this in turn has induced them to engage in self-criticism and transform their world outlooks. Here, as elsewhere, an effort has been made to apply Mao Tse-tung's directive: "In the construction of the socialist society, every individual must be remolded." This requirement applies to both young and inexperienced cadres.

An awareness of the scope of the changes that have occurred since 1966 is required for an understanding of the profound transformations that have been effected in management. The new organizational forms that emerged from the Cultural Revolution did not spring up full-blown. They resulted from an ideological class struggle extending over several years, and from a vast ideological effort to unify the masses. Even under these conditions, new types of organization were not easily developed.

The viability of the workers' management teams, for instance, is still under discussion, and there are other forms of workers' representation. All reflect the same general focus, however: to develop organizational structures affording the greatest possibilities for the masses to participate in running the factories and to make their weight felt. This in turn makes it possible to whittle down the administrative apparatus by simplifying the entire network of relations within the factory. Many problems in the shop are now settled on the spot.

A problem receiving much attention in current discussions involves the possibility that a gap may develop between the mass organizations and the masses themselves. There is indeed the danger that members of the workers' management teams or elected officials may eventually isolate themselves from the masses. A number of ideas are strongly emphasized in this connection: members of workers' management teams and similar organizations must make a persistent effort to raise their ideological level; they must be in the forefront of the movement for the study of Marxism-Leninism and Mao Tse-tung Thought; they must engage in productive labor; and their activities must be subjected to constant criticism by the masses. The fact that these cadres once earned the confidence of the workers does not guarantee that they will continue to follow a correct road. Their activities must therefore be reviewed periodically, and members of the workers' management teams and revolutionary committees may be discharged from their functions at the request of the workers. The most important check is that which comes from "below," but it must be complemented by a political check from the "top," instituted by the party committee.

The problem of the ideological revolutionization of the mass organizations is thus permanently on the agenda. The Chinese reject as illusory the belief that there are magic organizational formulas guaranteed to prevent any regression in a bourgeois direction.

2. Industrial Planning

State Property and Collective Property in Industry

There are two kinds of social property in China: state property and collective property; the second is owned by a specific collective of workers, such as a production brigade. The municipality of Shanghai, for instance, which extends beyond the city proper and encompasses all the suburbs, numbers about 9,800 enterprises and production units, of which 3,200 are owned by the state and 6,600 by collectives.

Viewed in terms of *management,* these enterprises can be divided into three categories:

1. Sizeable enterprises. These are under "state" management—under the control of the central government or provincial and municipal authorities.

2. Small urban enterprises. These are managed at the "street" or "neighborhood" level, generally under the direction of the corresponding revolutionary committee.

3. Industrial enterprises at the district, people's communes, and production brigade levels.

The first two categories serve the needs of the population, industry, and export, while the third serves *predominantly* the needs of agriculture, but also supplies some city factories (this is a marginal function). In the cities collectively owned industrial property exists at the "street" level, which involves production units managed within the confines of a residential block or street. In the suburbs collective property is owned primarily by people's communes and production brigades. In the municipality of Shanghai in 1971, for instance, industrial enterprises belonging to people's communes and production brigades (collective property) numbered 3,800; those under district management numbered 1,000. These three types of enterprise employed 280,000 people. The number of industrial workers in the municipality of Shanghai totaled 2.56 million.

The collective enterprises consist of small and medium-sized facilities. They are more numerous than the state factories but the value of their output is much lower: they account for only 4 percent of the value of industrial production, whereas state-owned facilities produce 96 percent.

The general tendency since 1957, and especially since the Cultural Revolution, has been to foster local initiative by decentralizing the management of state enterprises and giving local officials a free hand in managing a growing number of production units. The aggregate value produced under this type of management in Shanghai has developed as follows: In 1957 almost half (46 percent) of the value of industrial output originated in enterprises directly controlled by the central government. In 1970 only 6.8 percent of the value of industrial output originated in enterprises controlled by the central government, whereas *93.2 percent* of the value of industrial output originated in locally managed enterprises.

This decentralization is motivated by what the Chinese call the need to "struggle against the dictatorship of central management." This struggle is intended to foster a "twofold initiative"—that of the central government and that of local officials.

With respect to *size,* enterprises are considered big, medium-sized, or small. Small and medium-sized enterprises account for the bulk of production. Of the 3,200 state enterprises in Shanghai, only 90 can be considered big (most of these employ more than 3,000 workers), 300 are medium-sized, and 2,810 are small.

The distinction between big, medium-sized, and small

enterprises is not simply numerical; it also involves type of production. In the mechanical engineering industry, for instance, an enterprise is considered big if it employs more than 1,000 workers. In the textile industry, on the other hand, an enterprise is not considered big unless it employs at least 3,000 workers. In terms of size, the distribution of the total value of production in 1970 was as follows: big, 27.5 percent; medium-sized, 24.5 percent; small, 47 percent. In 1971, the figures were, respectively, 30 percent, 26 percent, and 44 percent.

The formation of people's communes was the point of departure for a substantial development of collective forms of property in industry.

The "street factories" are collective enterprises initiated by the inhabitants of a neighborhood or street and run by the neighborhood or street revolutionary committee. They emerged during the period of the Great Leap Forward, and were given a strong impetus by the Cultural Revolution. They represent a new type of industrial development and reflect an effort to destroy earlier forms. They also enable women to participate in the social labor of the community. In 1971 about 200,000 inhabitants of Shanghai worked in such enterprises; and almost all of them were initiated by housewives. These women had primarily political reasons for wanting to become involved in production: most of them were not financially obligated to supplement their husbands' incomes. They were motivated by their desire to engage in productive labor.[1]

The street factories engage in various types of production. They serve the immediate needs of the local population—mending clothes, sewing, laundering, odd repairs. They ease the burden of household work, thus enabling increasing numbers of housewives to become integrated in production.

1. On the social, ideological, and political role of the street and neighborhood enterprises, see Claudie Broyelle, *La Moitié du ciel* (Paris: Denoël-Gonthier, 1973).

They also meet wider needs—light machine work, manufacture of transistors, etc. These enterprises do not benefit
from state investment but depend entirely on marginal resources (waste materials, old machines, self-financing).

While these collective urban small enterprises at present
cater primarily to local needs, they attempt to meet wider
industrial needs and hope eventually to export their output.
In the districts and people's communes, the small enterprises
produce largely for agriculture (fertilizers, agricultural tools
and machinery, small vehicles, etc.), and sometimes for other
factories.

When one of these enterprises develops beyond a certain
size it becomes state property; such an outcome is regarded
as the crowning achievement of a successful effort. The factory is then directly integrated into the state plan. To cite
but one example, a Shanghai textile factory which worked
with cotton scraps has recently become a state factory.

Chinese economic policy attaches a great deal of importance to the development of small and medium-sized enterprises. Chinese industrial development rests chiefly upon
these enterprises. This approach should not be regarded as
motivated merely by economic necessity; it also reflects a
political choice. One of the major political advantages of
these enterprises consists in the fact that they permit a freer
development of the workers' management teams than is possible in big, complex enterprises imprinted with the capitalist
mode of production and its tendency toward hugeness. The
aim of the current political outlook is precisely to break up
or limit these giants and replace them with production units
that can be controlled by the workers.

Management and Planning in the State Sector

The base level of management is the factories themselves.
In Shanghai, for instance, these are supervised by bodies of
two types: industrial offices and specialized agencies.

The industrial offices specialize in the coordination of the various production units that turn out the same kind of product. Again using Shanghai as an example, there are nine such offices in that city. They specialize in iron and steel production, the production of other metals, chemicals, textiles and handicrafts, mechanical and electrical construction, electronic and telecommunication precision instruments, light industry, electric power, general construction (chiefly factories and housing, but also schools, hospitals, etc.). Each office supervises anywhere from a few dozen or a few hundred to between three hundred and six hundred factories.

The specialized agencies are controlled by the industrial offices; their area of responsibility is more limited—tractors, pharmaceuticals, etc. There are some one hundred specialized agencies in Shanghai. They act as intermediaries between the production units and the industrial offices. Some very important factories, however, are linked directly to the corresponding offices. The offices and agencies exercise both economic and political control over the enterprise with respect to planning. They intervene in the formation, institution, coordination, and implementation of the plan.

The very small number of enterprises directly accountable to the central government are controlled by a ministry which occupies an intermediate level between these enterprises and the government. To ensure unified planning on the provincial level, the plan for each province also encompasses the enterprises controlled by the central government. These enterprises are therefore not extraneous to the province; they receive aid in the planning of production and the allocation of their output from both the central government and the provincial revolutionary committee.

The local authorities (of provinces, districts, or municipalities) actually play a considerable role in planning and management. This decentralization enables the province or municipality to effect close cooperation between the various regional production units. Management at the provincial level is guided by a broad concept of relatively autonomous industrial development in each province; this promotes consistent development through the institution of complementary production facilities, and stimulates innovation and the search for local sources of raw materials.

Management at the provincial level seeks to coordinate the activities of the production units rather than stifle their initiative. In recent years, China was the scene of a struggle against centralization—the advocacy of centralization was a feature of Liu Shao-chi's line. In certain provinces, notably in the north, organizational structures similar to those of "trusts" had been instituted; they were eliminated during the Cultural Revolution.

Chinese decentralization is thus radically different from that practiced in the U.S.S.R. and the European "people's democracies," where it is characterized by the growing role of enterprise associations, a diminishing number of planned indices, etc. The political contexts are different. In current Soviet decentralization, power is shifting increasingly to the managers rather than to the workers. This decentralization in fact consists of a redistribution of powers within a state bourgeoisie. Viewed in terms of economic conditions, decentralization in the U.S.S.R. is combined with the erosion of price planning and an increasing stress on the role of profit. In China, on the other hand, decentralization is one of the factors enabling the workers to exercise collective control over their lives. Prices are planned and profit is not in command. The very methods of Chinese planning distinguish it from Soviet planning.

Decentralization accounts for the exceptional dynamism of the Chinese economy and for the sharp contraction of the administrative apparatus that can be observed everywhere. Such decentralization, moreover, constitutes one of the conditions for the development of socialist forms of management, and for workers' participation in management. It can be effectively combined with an economic plan only insofar as each enterprise subordinates its own interests to overall interests as spelled out in the plan. In the absence of this ideological condition, decentralization and planning are incompatible. There is then no other way but to issue peremptory and detailed orders, and to verify their implementation by bureaucratic means. We know what this leads to.

To designate a plan that is not administratively centralized, the Chinese use the term "unified planning." Its unified character is primarily political. It relies substantially on the initiative of the masses; its own role is an effort to foster and unify these initiatives.

The unified plan requires the implementation of principles that guide the workers both in the formulation of the plan and in management. At all levels, and in each production unit, the basic principles are the following: to put politics in command—to subordinate the interests of the factory as such to the collective interest and to the interests of the Chinese revolution; to rely on the initiative of the masses; to develop one's strength to the utmost; "to view agriculture as the base and industry as the dominant factor"; "to prepare against war and natural calamities, and everything for the people"; to follow the general line of socialist construction by applying the criteria of "quantity, speed, quality, economy"; and "to walk on two feet," which means to build both very simple factories and modern factories, big and small factories, and to use advanced and traditional techniques. The elaboration of the plan is also guided by the concrete (quantitative and qualitative) orientations given to different industries as a function of the general political line and the need for balanced overall development.

A unified plan means that the plans of the various production units must be unified; otherwise it becomes impossible to integrate the plans developed at different levels—the overall plan for the development of China, provincial plans, and local plans.

A number of products designated "primary products"—for instance, important raw materials such as coal and steel—

are planned directly at the national level. The plan for less important types of production (cement, furniture) is developed at the provincial level. In the case of still other products (farming implements, daily necessities), whose production is so dispersed as to make central planning pointless, the plan is elaborated at the district level. The output of the collective enterprises, which is destined largely for local consumption, falls into this category.

The national plan focuses first on the enterprises controlled directly by the central government. Production destined for export is also planned centrally. There is a monopoly on foreign trade in China. Import and export are the domain of state agencies which deal directly with the corresponding production units. Little information is available concerning the technical elaboration of the foreign trade plan, but the guiding principles are clear: to avoid placing excessive reliance on any one type of import; to provide aid to certain countries; to increase and diversify the number of trading partners.

The national plan does not encompass all the provincial and local plans in detail, but it does project the principal requirement of the various provinces. In the case of cement, for instance, the central plan indicates the quantities which the cement-producing provinces must furnish to other provinces. This requirement is incorporated into the provincial plan, which must meet the cement requirements of its own province and other provinces.

Even with respect to the allocation of the principal products, the state distribution agencies do not specify how each province or district is to employ the raw materials assigned to it. The same procedure is followed within each province. Each district receives indications as to its commitments to other districts. The various levels are thus coordinated flexibly, and not by means of abstract, rigid, and bureaucratic regulations.

The unified plan reflects a basic outlook: the need to

struggle against administrative centralism. Its aim is to establish conditions that will enable the immediate producers to exercise effective control over the means of production, rather than to keep them powerless, through the decisions of central offices instead of the mechanism of the market. Unified planning is an integral component of socialist construction.

The industrial production of consumer goods is planned primarily at the district or provincial level. The state plan and those of the various production units do not focus exclusively on production, but also on the allocation of output. Consumer goods are always distributed by state agencies of commerce, which play an essential role in elaborating and coordinating their planning. These agencies have a very important control function in that they represent the consumers with respect to the enterprises—the consumers' expressed wants are discussed at meetings between the enterprises and the agencies—and see to it that these wants are given full consideration. The production units conduct their own surveys and make every effort to keep in touch with the needs of the population. These investigations are carried out with the cooperation and aid of the state agencies of commerce. In projecting the exact quantity of the various products needed by the population, these state agencies compute such factors as rate of inventory turnover, daily product circulation, etc. Sounding out the consumers in regard to their wants helps the production units in their planning. These plans do not spell out in detail how a single product is to be diversified, however. The projection of product assortment is the responsibility of local management.

Samples of new products (such as footwear) are put on display so that the consumers may be questioned regarding their opinions and wants. Quantities are projected by the state agencies of commerce and adjusted in the course of the year. The production units also survey consumers' reaction to finished goods; they conduct inquiries in shops, homes, and work places, which help them to determine desirable modifications.

An example of how a product was modified as a result of an investigation into its practical use involves a factory which supplied a special type of raincoat to the people's communes. The factory workers arrived to conduct their investigation during the rice-planting season. They noticed that when they bent down, their raincoats dragged in the mud of the fields. Following discussions with the peasants, they altered the raincoats by adding a set of buttons that made it possible to raise the hem of the garment.

The mechanism of developing the plan—continuous exchanges between the base and the top—results in decisions arrived at in common. The party has the final say, but since matters are settled basically through discussion, any resulting contradictions are secondary contradictions. Chinese planning therefore has particular characteristics. The plan tries to rely to the utmost on the masses; it is not the exclusive concern of "experts." It is a political matter. It combines the political orientations—general line and specific directives – deriving from the party with the initiative of the masses. It is the focus of a maximum mobilization of all innovation efforts, and every attempt is made not to waste what the workers have produced. The role of the central administrative officials in the development and institution of the plan, while important in terms of the achievement of overall balance, is relatively limited. This kind of planning aims to develop productive forces resting on the associated workers—to initiate socialist cooperation.

Unity among socialist workers must develop on the basis of politics and ideology. Such a unity makes it possible to envisage the eventual elimination of the surviving market relations and the emergence of new socialist social relations, an outcome that is directly related to the ideological revolutionization achieved by the class struggle unfolding under the leadership of the Chinese Communist Party. The labor expended in production can thus become labor that is directly and genuinely social; it can gradually cease to be labor performed exclusively or principally for wages, and become labor expended essentially to satisfy social wants. The conception of the unified plan proceeding from the base serves the need for such a transformation.

The Development of the Unified Plan

The Factory Level

The plans are elaborated within a framework of a continuous exchange of opinions between the base and the top. The state—in this instance, the state planning committee—provides a few general indices to the various bureaus of the municipality of Peking (in this instance, the bureau of textiles), which in turn convey approximate indices to individual factories. These indices represent advisory norms. They are preliminary estimates established by the central government, the municipality, and the bureau of textiles, after consultations with the trade departments. They serve as the starting point for further development proceeding from the base—from within each factory.

The General Knitwear Factory in Peking has a productive capacity of 20 million items. The preliminary indices, which allow for the factory's capacity for production and diversification, are submitted for discussion by the workers. These discussions evaluate the factory machinery, innovations, and the creative initiative of the masses. The trade departments send their own teams to the factory where they present various marketing data. In the case of jackets, for instance, they set forth requirements regarding quantity, size, material—cotton, nylon, etc.—and style—type of collar, long or short sleeves, etc. Workers and factory employees visit stores and other outlets to obtain first-hand information concerning the views of the customers. Following a series of discussions in the workshops, a proposal is forwarded to the bureau of textiles of the Peking municipality.

In regard to products destined for export, the department concerned makes proposals which are also discussed by the masses, following which the factory presents counter-proposals. The planning agency coordinates all the data in terms of the need to assure an overall balance and establishes definitive indices in consultation with the factory. The decisions taken by the planning agency are then transmitted to the factory.

There is an annual industrial plan, and it can be broken down into monthly and quarterly plans. These may be modified in keeping with fluctuations in market need. The annual production goals can be modified, if necessary, to prevent the production of superfluous products. Such decisions are made by the planning agency. Within the factory itself, it is the production team supervised by the revolutionary committee which deals concretely with the implementation of the annual plan.

The General Knitwear Factory operates largely on an annual plan, but the factory also makes proposals for the five-year plans. Some of the principal norms used in the preparation of the plan are: aggregate value, quantity of the chief types of production, costs, profit, labor productivity, quality, product design and range. There are also norms concerning labor power, raw materials, etc. All these factors are passed under regular review during the implementation of the plan.

The plan and the evaluations bear not only on the goals to be attained and the norms to be observed, but also on specific measures to be taken. How should the various tasks be accomplished? What changes should be made in the machines, in the procurement of supplies, in the stocks of raw materials? Every effort is made to solve problems on the spot with the help of campaigns to promote technical revolutionization, so as to conserve raw materials, upgrade the machinery, increase productivity, and improve quality.

The Provincial Level

The province of Liaoning has a population of 28 million, two-thirds of whom live in the countryside and one-third in the towns. There are about 2.4 million workers in the province.

Heavy industry used to be dominant. At present, in keeping with the basic directive regarding the need for the relatively autonomous development of each province, industrial production has been diversified in the older as well as in the new branches of industry. The province now produces a wide variety of industrial products—iron and steel, machinery, coal, oil, electricity, electrical engineering products, textiles, clothing, shoes, furniture, etc. Agriculture has also been developed and diversified. Industrial production represents 90 percent of the aggregate value of the production of the province, whereas agricultural production accounts for 10 percent.

On the subject of agriculture, a member of the Liaoning revolutionary committee gave the following explanation:

"Current agricultural production in the province is probably adequate for our needs. In the municipality of Shen-yang, which has the highest urban concentration in the province—60 percent urban and 40 percent rural population—cereal and vegetable production is now adequate. Previously we had to import 800 million *jin* [880 million lbs.] of cereal annually. Last year, after a two-year effort, we managed to produce enough for our needs. We used to have to import some vegetables from Canton and a northern province. As of last year, production is adequate to meet the needs of the town's population, and we can even do some exporting. Vegetable production has reached 1.5 billion *jin,* or 1.65 billion pounds.

These facts prove that in spite of the size of the urban population we were able to produce the cereals and vegetables we need without neglecting our industrial potential."

Concerning the plan, this member provided the following information:

"In the area of planning we are currently at the stage of struggle-criticism-reform. Liu Shao-chi's revisionist line—which advocated putting profit in command, using material incentives, the domination of experts, and relied heavily on foreigners—is being refuted. In factory production we are not concerned exclusively with profit; our basic approach is to consider the needs of the national economy.

"To increase production, we must rely chiefly on political and ideological work so as to ensure that everybody works for the revolution, to serve the people, and not for material incentives. To achieve the success of the plan, we rely on the three-in-one combination of workers, technicians, and cadres, and not on a small number of specialists."

The plan is developed in several stages. The production units are given general guidelines reflecting estimates of social needs. These guidelines do not include precise figures but rather the orders of priority and magnitude. The initial elaboration of the plan takes place in each production unit, and is guided by the principle of "mobilizing the masses." One point is often stressed: it is necessary to be realistic, to maintain sufficient latitude, to anticipate obstacles. It is necessary to be both bold and modest.

To obtain concrete data regarding the wants of the consumers or users, the workers conduct their own investigations. The workers of an agricultural machinery factory, for instance, will investigate the situation in the people's communes so as to become familiar with their machinery requirements. When several factories are interested in the same type of product, delegates from these factories meet to discuss the most judicious way of allocating the products among them. The results of the investigations and discussions are reviewed by the revolutionary committees, workers' management teams, and three-in-one teams of each factory.

These planning projects must then be coordinated. The coordination agencies vary with the nature of the products and the area of consumption. Depending on the case, the official bodies participating in the discussions consist of the district revolutionary committee or the provincial revolutionary committee, and in the case of very large industries, of the central government.

The political and administrative officials concerned review and coordinate the projects, and establish a balance between resources and requirements. This process, during which contact is maintained with the various production units, results in the development of an overall planning project which encompasses the partial projects. This planning project is forwarded to the production units concerned and is again discussed by the workers.

A member of the Liaoning revolutionary committee described the procedure as follows: "First, from the base to the top; second, a combination of top and base—the 'top' does not operate in a void, but contacts the various production units with a view to elaborating a new planning project; third, a combination relying principally on the efforts of the province; fourth, a combination of the efforts of both the provinces and the central government."

The requirements of the state—those deriving from the central government and reflecting the requirements of the other provinces, of the People's Liberation Army, etc.—are forwarded to the various provinces and incorporated in the plan of each province. The individual provincial plan also incorporates the dependable resources available from the other provinces. The overall approach is always to try to make the provinces and districts relatively autonomous.

Given the conditions under which the plan is elaborated and the fact that people try to be modest, it should be noted that the plans are in most cases not only fulfilled, but over-fulfilled. When it is clear that a plan cannot be fulfilled, however, there is a discussion to determine which of the projected goals is to be abandoned. The choices are made in close consultation with the masses during the implementation of the plan.

The tendency before the Cultural Revolution was to leave all these problems in the hands of experts and managers. In spite of mass criticism, this tendency has not yet been entirely eliminated. In one instance, the members of a factory revolutionary committee considered the plan impossible to fulfill and wanted to scale it down without consulting the masses. The workers criticized the managers of this factory. When the difficulties were reexamined, solutions were found and, owing to the measures suggested in the course of discussions with the workers, the initial objectives were eventually attained.

During both elaboration and execution of the plan, the problem constantly arises of establishing a balance between the requirements of consumer needs and those of productive consumption. The method of automatically lowering the projected production goals is rejected; the emphasis is on searching out solutions that will make it possible to reach the initial objectives. This is called the search for an "active balance" rather than a "passive balance." It is also said that imbalances are handled positively and not negatively. This is done in consultation with the workers. In this connection, a member of the Liaoning revolutionary committee made this comment:

"In last year's plan, coal posed a problem. The alternatives were to make our projections in terms of actual coal production and therefore to narrow the plan's objectives with respect to other products, or to mobilize the masses with a view toward increasing coal production. The workers met many times to discuss the matter. They concluded that since there was not enough coal it was necessary to appeal to the masses to increase coal production and economize on its use.

"The masses were informed of the lack of coal and of the resulting situation. As soon as the facts were known, the workers began to exert their efforts. Coal production in the province increased by several million tons. The savings realized were also on the order of several million tons. Industrial activity could thus depend on the necessary fuel for the development of production, and the state plan was fulfilled. This shows that it is better to rely on the initiative of the masses than on slide rules."

The Five-Year Plan

Five-year plans are much less detailed than the annual plans but they are elaborated according to the same principles. They provide general guidelines concerning the desired growth of essential types of production. They do not project detailed objectives for each production unit—this is considered unnecessary and unrealistic. When the establishment of very large production units is envisaged, however, more detailed projects are formulated in close consultation with the workers familiar with the industry in question. This kind of effort is not limited to "experts" but involves mass participation.

The five-year plans also encompass far-reaching projects for the renovation and enlargement of the production units. The choice of the factories to be renovated or enlarged is made in consultation with the production units themselves. Within a given branch of industry, the political officials and production units together determine which of these units can benefit most effectively from expansion or renovation. Final selections are made only after comprehensive discussion with the workers of the enterprises in question.

The details of the projects are the subject of mass discussion within the enterprises. Eventually there are also discussions with the workers of other factories, especially with those in the production units that are to supply the necessary equipment for the enlargement or renovation projects. These consultations are very close, and if necessary involve exchanges of workers among the various enterprises so that they may become familiar with local conditions.

Insofar as the work of elaborating the plan is done in close consultation with the workers and is based on a careful and concrete examination of the situation with a view toward establishing realistic and modest objectives, its successful accomplishment does not in principle meet with major difficulties. And since the workers participate in elaborating the plan and play a key role in formulating its goals, they are justified in regarding its successful outcome as "their affair" and in exerting all their efforts to attain its objectives. It is nevertheless impossible to develop all aspects of the plan at the same pace: everything during the year does not happen exactly as anticipated; difficulties and problems inevitably crop up. Every effort is made to solve these problems on the spot with the help of the workers. It is only as a last resort that help is requested from other production units, or that the district or provincial revolutionary committee is asked to lower the objectives.

When, in spite of everything, the plan cannot be realized in its entirety, the problem arises as to which objectives are to be abandoned. In keeping with the principle of stressing the need to satisfy overall needs, priority is generally given to tasks involving meeting the requirements of the other provinces.

A member of the Nanking revolutionary committee explained: "Priority must be given to achieving a balance at the national level; without a national equilibrium, a provincial balance is impossible." The application of this principle, however, is subject to a concrete examination of whether the course adopted might result in major difficulties in the province.

At any rate, no decision regarding the lowering of production can be made by the factory itself. Factory plans apparently are scaled down only in exceptional cases. This is due to the realism of China's economic plans and to the direct contacts between the workers of the various production units engaged in the manufacture of the same product. These close relationships play a decisive role in helping resolve the concrete problems that arise whenever there is a danger that a partial objective of the plan may not be attained.

The Relations Between Production Units

The production units maintain contact not only indirectly through the corresponding bureaus but also directly, especially through close relations between the workers of these factories. Efforts are pooled in a search for solutions to whatever problems arise. These direct relationships are a concrete example of socialist cooperation.

The existence of very close contacts between the various production units in no way signifies that they maintain direct market relations, however. Prices are planned and fixed outside the factories. The allocation of products among the enterprises is made by the state agencies of commerce, which also channel the products to the individual consumers. This is very important in terms of preventing the development of exchanges that bear no relationship to the plan.

The Question of Planned Prices

Prices play a rather secondary role in the Chinese economy. Monetary calculation intended to "maximize" the income of each production unit is not a dominant factor in the formulation of planning objectives at the overall level or at the level of a particular production unit. This does not mean that no effort is made to estimate and reduce costs, but prices do not direct production. Production is determined by the political line. The prices themselves are secondary expressions of the political line.

There is an essential preoccupation with price stability and overall financial balance. Prices must be stable and the production units must rely as little as possible on public financial resources to make up any deficit; for the production units to be in the red could only lead to an unhealthy situation. On the contrary, the profits of the production units are placed at the service of overall economic development.

In practice, to speak of stable prices is tantamount to saying that the prevailing prices are largely either "historically given prices" or prices adjusted for political reasons and in keeping with cost variations. The selling prices in each industry are fixed on the basis of cost prices. The selling price to the state agencies of commerce generally equals the average cost price, to which a 15 percent margin is added; the amount represented by this margin is added to the social accumulation fund. The selling price to the consumers is fixed according to a variety of policies.

1. There is no profit on essential goods; if necessary they are subsidized by the state. In the case of cereals, for instance, which are under state monopoly, the purchase price from the peasants practically equals the retail price. This means that the state assumes the cost of marketing, transportation, etc. In certain regions, such as the north, where the cost price of cereals (the purchase price from the people's communes) is higher, the retail selling price has nevertheless remained the same as elsewhere. On these products, therefore, the agencies of commerce sustain a loss.

On the whole, the price to the consumers of certain essential foods has in recent years been lowered without a decrease in the purchase price from the people's communes. The selling price of 50 kg. of rice, for instance, decreased from 17.63 yuan in 1950 to 16.40 yuan in 1970. Similarly, the purchase price from the people's communes may be increased without an increase in the selling price to the consumers; this happened last year in the case of rapeseed and rape oil.

2. Products essential to the health of the people are sold

at cost price, which means that no profit is made on their sale. The price of medicine, for instance, has decreased in keeping with reduced cost price. Thus the price of 200,000 units of penicillin decreased from 2.10 yuan in 1953 to 1.23 yuan in 1970. When a social need is given priority, price gives way to free distribution, as in the case of birth-control devices.

3. Everyday necessities are cheap, although a profit margin is maintained. The price of 50 kg. of lump coal, for instance, decreased from 2.80 yuan to 2.50 yuan between 1950 and 1970.

4. In the case of nonessential products (transistor radios, cameras, etc.), the "historically given price" is generally maintained. Any eventual drop in the cost price of these products serves to increase the social accumulation fund.

The main thing is to understand that China's approach to prices involves not merely policies, but politics—it rests on political and social choices.

In brief, consumer goods may be divided into three main categories: (1) those corresponding to essential needs—these are sold at the lowest possible price; (2) those corresponding to less essential needs—their price to the consumer is higher than their cost price, but is lowered as the cost price decreases; and (3) those currently viewed as corresponding to secondary needs—their prices remain the same. On the whole, therefore, not only are prices not rising, they are getting lower.

The price of equipment, raw materials, energy, etc., supplied to the production units is based on cost price. Here, too, every effort is made to maintain price stability, and if a cost price goes down this decrease is not automatically reflected in the selling price to the production units. The drop in cost price is reflected in growing profits for the producing factories and not in reduced costs for the industrial consumer. If the drop in cost price is considerable, however, it is passed on to the industrial consumer, but this is not done while an annual plan is operative, so as not to invalidate the comparison between effective cost price and planned cost price. The savings realized by enterprises that paid less than expected for their supplies would be due not to efforts on their part, but to the lower cost of raw materials. For each production unit to be able to evaluate its operation, it is preferable that prices be stable. In any case, the determination of what is to be produced and how production is to take place (techniques used, raw materials utilized, etc.) depends only secondarily on monetary competition. The basic decisions reflect the pressing needs of overall economic development. They are not subordinated to monetary computations such as could be made by individual production units.

Socialist Cooperation

Socialist cooperation between factories requires that an enterprise be as concerned with the interests of the surrounding population and those of the enterprises or consumers for which it produces as with its own particular interests. Following are two examples of such cooperation.

The first concerns the struggle against pollution, which has achieved spectacular results in such large cities as Tientsin and Shanghai, owing to the cooperation of the various enterprises and of the population. This cooperation has made it possible in these cities to divert waste waters from the rivers, dig underground canals, and build factories for the transformation of these waters. These factories salvage thousands of tons of useful products and produce fertilizers that are used over tens of thousands of acres of land.

Significant results have also been obtained in the treatment of rubbish, solid wastes, and residual gases, which have been transformed into new raw materials. In the Fouchoun area of Liaoning the treatment of residual gas, waste water, and slag originating in Oil Refinery No. 3 has produced nineteen chemical products and rare metals. As a result of changes introduced in the operation of the refinery, the surrounding atmosphere has been purified and raw materials valued at several million yuan are now obtained each year. They include sodium, sulphates, dry ice, raw materials for the manufacture of synthetic textiles, and so on.

The second example concerns the search for product quality and durability through close cooperation between the industrial producers and the industrial users as well as between the producing industries and the consumers. This cooperation has resulted in considerable achievements, which are confirmed by the industrial and agricultural users, the people involved in the distribution network, and the individual buyers. These achievements serve the interests of the consumers rather than those of the producers. For the producing enterprises, improving the quality, solidity, and durability of their products generally represents a great deal of extra work (research, development, etc.) and eventually rising costs. These improvements, however, do not automatically entail higher prices or increased total sales; the contrary is true when products become more durable.

The producing enterprises thus subordinate their particular interests to the overall interests of the country. This is the driving force of a new kind of economic progress—production is no longer dominated by the pursuit of exchange value, growth, monetary returns and profit, but by the pursuit of use value. This presupposes radical transformations in social relations, in the economic base as well as in the superstructure.

Contrary to certain views which claim Marxism as their authority but reject its basic ideas, such transformations *are not spontaneous.* They are not *mechanistically determined* by the development of the productive forces. Consequently— and this point is essential for an understanding of the Great Proletarian Cultural Revolution and its significance—it should be considered that the transformations in the economic base which can be currently observed in China must of necessity result from a struggle which has been waged, and continues to be waged, by the workers to transform the social division of labor, eliminate hierarchical relations within the production units, take management into their own hands, and master technology. This is a political and ideological struggle. It is not a mere revolt. It has a revolutionary character. Its success requires a unity of conception and action, and a correct estimate of the nature of viable transformations and their interdependence. This is why such a struggle demands the leadership of a revolutionary party.

3. Transformations in the Social Division of Labor

Administrative Tasks and Performance Tasks

A first set of observations bears on the significant changes which have been initiated in recent years, and which are designed to further the withering of the social division of labor and foster a new approach to the development of the productive forces. These changes have crucial implications, for they concern the production relations themselves—the relations of the agents of production among themselves and with the means of production. Socialism, however, signifies not only, nor even primarily, a change in the juridical relations of ownership; such a change may be purely formal. Socialism implies also, and above all, a change in the relations of production.

It is clearly impossible to examine all the features of the transformations that first emerged on a significant scale during the period of the Great Leap Forward, and were then greatly extended under the impetus of the Cultural Revolution. We will discuss only a few essential features of these transformations.

One aspect of these transformations bears on the division between administrative tasks and performance tasks. While the distinction between these certainly continues to exist, the division among those who carry them out has tended to become obliterated largely through the expanding activities of the three-in-one teams. These transformations correspond to an unquestionable revolutionization of the industrial enterprises and are laying the foundations for a transition from management by a minority to management by the majority, or *mass management.*

In this connection, we will now discuss the state factories; the industrial enterprises run by the people's communes have a somewhat different status and are therefore not included in this study. By "state factories" are meant factories run either directly by the central government or by the revolutionary committees of a province, district, or municipality, which represent the state power at these three levels.[1] All these factories are part of the state sector, even when they are not administered by a central ministry but by a district (whose population is about 500,000).

Before the Cultural Revolution the factories in the state sector were administered by the party committee and managed in their day-to-day operation by a director who quite often seems to have assumed both functions. In those days the director was not elected by the workers but appointed by the administrative department which supervised the factory.[2] The composition of the party committee was in principle determined by the party members in the factory itself, but in actual fact the party committee was very frequently designated by high party officials.

In 1960 this type of organization, which excludes the participation of the masses, was criticized by Mao Tse-tung. On March 22, 1960, he proclaimed in its place the Anshan Constitution, which was inspired by the experience of the Great Leap Forward and by the initiatives undertaken at that time by the workers of the Anshan metallurgical combine. This constitution states some of the conditions required for the

1. For the state power to be represented by committees all of whose members are elected and recallable by the masses signifies a step forward in the direction of the withering away of the state (see Marx's writings on the Paris Commune).

2. See C. Bettelheim, J. Charrière, and H. Marchisio, *La Construction du socialisme en Chine* (Paris: Maspero, 1965); also in the *Petite Collection Maspero*.

socialist management of enterprises, notably in the form of five basic principles.[3]

The constitution stresses that politics must be put in command, that the workers must participate in management, and that cadres must engage in manual labor; these principles were reappropriated and implemented by the masses at the outset of the Cultural Revolution. The Anshan Constitution opposes the management practices that prevailed in 1960 and continued to prevail until the Cultural Revolution. It represents the starting point for a new social practice. As long as the masses had not begun to move on a broad scale, and had not themselves dealt with all these problems, the old state of affairs continued to exist.

It took eight years for the revolutionary committee of the Anshan municipality to adopt an official resolution which made the Anshan Constitution the basis for the organization of all the enterprises in the region. This resolution was adopted in Anshan on May 22, 1968. It represents the culmination of a mass movement whose initiatives were thus ratified by the revolutionary committee. The delay in adopting and instituting principles set forth by Mao Tse-tung himself was due to the fact that the proposed new mode of management had revolutionary implications. It required the launching of a class struggle and a broad mass movement; this is precisely what happened during the Cultural Revolution.

Mao Tse-tung did not attempt to change the situation "from the top," an approach which could only have resulted in superficial changes.[4] A revolutionary leadership cannot

3. See "The Constitution of the Anshan Iron and Steel Company Stimulates the Revolution of Production," in *Peking Review,* April 17, 1970. The basic principles of this constitution have been summarized in Chapter 1.

4. The policy of relying on the masses is a constant feature of the entire prior practice of Mao Tse-tung and the Chinese Communist Party. By way of example see the following passage from Mao Tse-tung's directive of October 1, 1943: "As rent reduction is a mass struggle by the peasants, party directives and government decrees should guide and help it instead of trying to bestow favours on the

substitute itself for the workers. According to the great principle of the *Communist Manifesto,* the mass movement must itself shatter the old relations: "The emancipation of the workers must be the act of the workers themselves." The state of affairs that existed in 1960 could be changed only through the initiative and revolutionary criticism of the masses, especially since the advocates of the capitalist road—the adherents of Liu Shao-chi—tried to preserve the then prevailing forms of management.

The period 1960-1966 witnessed a struggle between two lines, during which the Anshan Constitution was set aside. Generally speaking, the proponents of the capitalist road favored modes and principles of management similar to those prevailing in the U.S.S.R.; these are the principles that underlie what the Chinese call the "Magnitogorsk Constitution" (in contrast to the Anshan Constitution), which is meant to designate the management methods applied in the Soviet iron and steel combine at Magnitogorsk.

In their characteristic succinct style, the Chinese describe the earlier form of organization as "factory management by experts who put production in the forefront and tended to put profits in command." This was paralleled by a stress on material incentives—bonuses, growing wage differentiation, etc.—all of which are prevalent in the U.S.S.R. The same tendencies were at work in China before the Cultural Revolution, although in much less developed form.

The proponents of the revisionist line offered considerable resistance. The then prevailing forms of management in fact enabled a minority to benefit from its dominant position in

---

masses. To bestow rent reduction as a favour instead of arousing the masses to achieve it by their own action is wrong, and the results will not be solid." "Spread the Campaigns to Reduce Rent, Increase Production and 'Support the Government and Cherish the People' in the Base Areas," *Selected Works,* vol. III (Peking: Foreign Languages Press, 1965), p. 131.

relation to the means of production, and from its privileged position in the decision-making process—formation and utilization of the accumulation fund, substance and implementation of the plan, technical changes, allocation of tasks, determination of regulations, etc.

Resistance to the replacement of prevailing forms of management with socialist forms of management was especially prolonged since it emanated not only from the "experts" in the enterprises, but also from individuals within the Communist Party, some of whom were at a level close to that of the central leadership and were part of what has been described as a "general headquarters of the bourgeoisie" that had been constituted around Liu Shao-chi. In addition, the distortion of the revolutionary line by the "ultra-left" (see Postscript) undermined the implementation of this line. Whereas the revolutionary line, for instance, held that it was necessary to envisage the integration of the technicians and experts into the three-in-one teams, the "ultra-left" advocated their elimination. Many workers refused to accept this approach and the institution of new forms of management was delayed. To be sure, the struggle against the bourgeois line—against both its right and left manifestations—continues.

Finally, the opposition constantly reiterated its claim that its stand conformed to Soviet practice—not only during this period, but even prior to the Twentieth Congress.

The principles of the absolute authority of the director, of the privileged role of experts and specialists, and of the need to stress bonuses and material rewards are not confined to current management practice in the Soviet Union. These principles were implemented in Russia under the difficult conditions that prevailed after the October Revolution, especially during the period of War Communism. They were maintained under the New Economic Policy, and received a strong impetus during the period of rapid industrialization that followed in the wake of the first five-year plans.

The notion that a director should be solely responsible for

the implementation of party policy and thus have absolute authority in the factory had been advocated by Lenin in March 1918. This view of management, and the reliance on bourgeois specialists and a system of bonuses, met with strong objections from opposition tendencies within the Bolshevik Party, but these objections were never more than those of feeble minorities.

In Lenin's view, granting specialists an administrative role— and high salaries—was not in keeping with a "proletarian approach." He regarded this step as a necessary retreat imposed by the circumstances surrounding the construction of new social relations. In his words:

> It is clear that this measure not only implies the cessation—in a certain field and to a certain degree—of the offensive against capital (for capital is not a sum of money, but a definite social relation); it is also *a step backward* on the part of our socialist Soviet state power, which from the very outset proclaimed and pursued the policy of reducing high salaries to the level of the wages of the average worker.[5]

What was involved, as Lenin saw it, was indeed a retreat, a "step backward," which he made no attempt to disguise: the Soviet power temporarily entrusted administrative tasks to specialists and agreed to pay them high salaries. In fact, this step backward was never followed by a step forward. In the course of time the social extraction of the specialists underwent a change. The specialists of bourgeois origin gave way to men of working-class origin, but these new specialists were placed in the same relations of administration and authority; this means that in this area the policy of taking a "step backward" in the offensive against capital, which is a "definite social relation," has not been reversed.

Lenin also demanded the adoption of work norms:

5. Lenin, "The Immediate Tasks of the Soviet Government," *Selected Works*, vol. 2 (Moscow: Progress Publishers, 1967), p. 655.

The task that the Soviet government must set the people in all its scope is—learn to work. The Taylor system, the last word of capitalism in this respect, like all capitalist progress, is a combination of the refined brutality of bourgeois exploitation and a number of the greatest scientific achievements in the field of analysing mechanical motions during work, the elimination of superfluous and awkward motions, the elaboration of correct methods of work, the introduction of the best system of accounting and control, etc. The Soviet Republic must at all costs adopt all that is valuable in the achievements of science and technology in this field. The possibility of building socialism depends exactly upon our success in combining the Soviet power and the Soviet organisation of administration with the up-to-date achievements of capitalism. We must organise in Russia the study and teaching of the Taylor system and systematically try it out and adapt it to our own ends. At the same time, in working to raise the productivity of labour, we must take into account the specific features of the transition period from capitalism to socialism, which, on the one hand, require that the foundations be laid of the socialist organisation of competition, and, on the other hand, require the use of compulsion, so that the slogan of the dictatorship of the proletariat shall not be desecrated by the practice of a lily-livered proletarian government.[6]

For Lenin, who wrote these lines while Russia was in chaos and the party was incapable of fostering genuine proletarian discipline, this was again to be a temporary measure. But this temporary measure became a permanent feature. On the whole, the system of norms and bonuses remained dominant and was carried to very great lengths during the five-year plans.

In "The Immediate Tasks of the Soviet Government," Lenin argues that associate administration, which in his view promotes irresponsibility, must be replaced with administration by a single individual:

6. Ibid., p. 664.

But how can strict unity of will be ensured? By thousands subordinating their will to the will of one.

Given ideal class-consciousness and discipline on the part of those participating in the common work, this subordination would be something like the mild leadership of a conductor of an orchestra. It may assume the sharp forms of a dictatorship if ideal discipline and class-consciousness are lacking. But be that as it may, *unquestioning subordination* to a single will is absolutely necessary for the success of processes organised on the pattern of large-scale machine industry. On the railways [where the situation was particularly chaotic—C. B.] it is twice and three times as necessary. In this transition from one political task to another, which *on the surface* is totally dissimilar to the first, lies the whole originality of the present situation. The revolution has only just smashed the oldest, strongest and heaviest of fetters, to which the people submitted under duress. That was yesterday. Today, however, the same revolution demands—precisely in the interests of its development and consolidation, precisely in the interest of socialism—that the people *unquestioningly obey the single will* of the leaders of labour.[7]

Lenin's views may have corresponded to the requirements of a specific stage of the Russian Revolution, but once adopted (between 1918 and 1922) and implemented, they were never abandoned. On the contrary, the weight and authority of the factory director and of the factory party secretary—authority which is not subject to review by the workers—have become more powerful over the years. In fact, the consolidation in the factory of the relations of authority and command between administration, cadres, specialists, and technicians on the one hand, and the direct producers on the other, has provided fertile ground for the growth of Soviet revisionism.

Mao Tse-tung has rejected such forms of management and has on more than one occasion stressed his belief that "historical experience deserves attention." In China, factory

7. Ibid., p. 673 (italics in original).

management is primarily *political* management, which gives priority to the *political* objectives of socialist construction and not to narrow economic objectives. In carrying out their management task, the revolutionary committees are under the leadership of the factory party committee. The party committee, too, is now much more subject to control by the masses than previously, for the factory party organizations generally hold meetings that are attended by representatives of the masses.

Through the workers' management teams and the revolutionary committees a start has been made toward the end of eliminating the distinction and division between administrative and performance tasks. This process involves various forms of management by the workers and the participation of the cadres in manual labor.

This tendency is not limited to the presence of a few delegates in the revolutionary committees, and to the control of the revolutionary and party committees by the workers. First, all those who have managerial and administrative responsibilities must spend two or three days a week in manual labor, generally at a specific job. Second, managerial and control activities *have been reduced at the level of the workshops, sections of the shops, and work teams,* owing to the formation of workers' management teams, and work team and workshop assemblies, and teams for the study and application of Mao Tse-tung Thought. The activities of all these groups focus on the most diverse aspects of factory life—elaboration of production plans, delineation of production tasks, computation of costs, innovations and investments, establishment of work and safety regulations, management of the welfare fund, etc. According to available data, the proportion of the workers regularly involved in these various types of activity is about 20 percent, but the other workers also intervene in these activities through such instruments as the shop and work team assemblies.

To be sure, the expansion of these activities was made

possible by the politicization of the masses and the increasing prevalence of a proletarian morality. Thus the factory is less and less a simple production unit preoccupied with limited and narrowly technical problems, and more and more clearly a political unit and the site of intense ideological activity.

Intellectual Labor and Manual Labor

The division between manual labor and intellectual labor in a capitalist factory is reflected in the distinction between the immediate production work assigned to the workers and the tasks of the engineers and technicians who supervise production processes and make decisions regarding changes in work procedures, the utilization of machines, technical rules, etc. When this division is maintained or grows sharper, as is the case in capitalist factories, it places the immediate producers in a subordinate position with respect to the engineers and technicians. The transformations that occurred during the Cultural Revolution signify that a struggle is being waged in China to eliminate this aspect of the division of labor as well.

One of the outcomes of this struggle has been the formation of what the Chinese call three-in-one combination teams, teams charged with technical questions and consisting of workers, technicians, and cadres. According to a formulation widely used in China, the workers are the backbone of these teams, their leading force. The three-in-one teams take charge of the technical transformation of the factories, technical renovation, innovations and changes in technical regulations, and the struggle against the "unreasonable rules" that existed in these areas. Because of these "unreasonable rules," only engineers and technicians had the privilege of modifying machines.

The activities of the three-in-one teams, political and ideological education, and the integration of the engineers in manual labor, are gradually obliterating the separation between engineers and technicians on the one hand and workers on the other, as well as the domination of the workers by the technicians and engineers. This trend is reinforced by the profound transformation of the system of education, a complex task which is far from complete, requiring both time and experimentation in the resolution of problems.

Close links have been established between education and production work. The new technicians and engineers come straight from production; after completing the general course they spend two or three years as workers, peasants, or members of the People's Liberation Army (soldiers are also directly involved in production). Their fellow workers then select those who are to continue their studies (with their consent, of course); the choice is based on the candidate's overall practice and not only on intellectual criteria. The basic criterion is willingness to serve the people—to acquire knowledge not for personal advantage but for use in the service of the people. Admission to the university involves three steps: an individual request for admission, the designation of fellow workers, and a determination of the course of work in terms of the student's capacity and the needs of his or her production unit. Students keep in close touch with their workplace.

The old forms of the division of labor are obviously still far from completely shattered. Certain kinds of work are more attractive than others, but the less appealing jobs are increasingly being integrated into collective tasks which enable each individual to play a clearly useful and active role. Workers also have numerous possibilities for learning new skills, not only through the engineering schools, but also because of the reorganization of the production processes and the various ways in which the factory itself provides professional training opportunities. The effort to make work less fragmentary by modifying its conditions and enabling each worker to master part of the production process is also very important. The assembly line must not dominate the worker; increasingly, it is the worker who is setting its pace.

The process of revolutionizing the mode of work is of necessity a long one—but it has been partially initiated through recognition of the fact that specific forms of the division of labor do not result from an abstract development of the productive forces, but that a work mode results from a transformation of the relations of production by past or present class struggles.

The transformations designed to eliminate the division between manual labor and intellectual labor are of decisive importance in achieving progress along the road to socialism. Generally speaking, they signify that one of the most profound characteristics of all class societies—the social separation between theory and practice—is in the process of being eliminated. In the capitalist mode of production this separation manifests itself concretely in the accumulation of both scientific and technical theoretical knowledge, and "practical" knowledge. The former assumes the form of sciences and technologies supposedly represented exclusively by scientists, engineers, and technicians; "practical" knowledge is reduced to mere routine or simple tricks of the trade.

Although the sciences and techniques have assumed an *apparently* autonomous guise which has given a considerable impulse to the development in knowledge, their growing separation from the practice of material production nevertheless produces contradictory social effects: it tends to deprive the immediate producers of knowledge that could enrich their practice of production and enable them to transform it themselves. Concurrently, this separation deprives the engineers, and especially the scientists, of useful practical types of knowledge. The social affirmation of the primacy of practice thus has considerable implications in China; it profoundly affects the reproduction of scientific and technical knowledge, the apparent autonomy of which can thus be torn up by the roots.

One of the effects of the separation between the sciences and techniques and the practice of production, contrary to what one might think, is the conservative character of technique. The illusion of the primacy of theory tends to arouse enormous social resistance to technical changes suggested by workers, especially when these changes contradict the ideas sanctioned by scientists and technicians. The Cultural Revolution in China has shown how thousands of innovations had previously been blocked by technicians who viewed them as inconsistent with the scientific and technical concepts they had been taught. The notion of the primacy of theory, which reflects bourgeois concepts and the capitalist division of labor, thus tends to render "unacceptable" any production method or technical change that is considered "technically invalid," thereby fostering theoretical conservatism.

In China today the relation between abstract knowledge in its theoretical form and the practice of production is being increasingly modified problems are no longer "settled" through appeal to theory alone. There is concrete evidence to show that when the primacy of practice is socially acknowledged, a whole range of transformations that cannot as yet be synthesized theoretically can nevertheless be incorporated into practice; this accelerates technical change and gives rise to a new type of technical development. (In the altogether different domain of medicine, for example, the use of acupuncture is a striking example of how practice can take a "lead" over theory.) The three-in-one teams directed by the workers provide a concrete social basis for this kind of development of technique and industrial production. These teams have made it possible to achieve a considerable number of technical innovations which bear not only on the production of new machinery, but also on the transformation of existing machines. Machines are no longer viewed as immutable objects, but as subject to modification by the workers themselves.

The innovations and technical renovations impelled by the

three-in-one teams often produce as much as a threefold increase in the productive capacity of old machines. This affects the economic potential, since it makes possible a rapid growth in the productive capacity of the existing machines, and a development of the productive forces that requires minimal prior accumulation.

In addition to affecting the transformation of technique, the three-in-one teams are also transforming the relations of the workers to their means of production. The expanding activities of the three-in-one teams are occurring in a context of class struggle. Technology is never neutral; it is never above or beside the class struggle. The class struggle, and the changes it imposes on the production process and production relations, ultimately determines the specific character of the productive forces and of their development. The socialist transformation of the production processes thus fosters the progressive obliteration of the social *separation* between scientific and technical activities and directly productive activities. This transformation also presupposes that—contrary to the practice of capitalist countries—the achievement of innovations is not subordinated to the possibility of selling new products or new services yielding increasing profits. China has eliminated this subordination and thus cleared the way for a vast expansion of innovation and renovation, of technical changes many of which result not in the construction of new machines or new factories but in the transformation and perfecting of existing machines or factories.

Socially, scientific and technical activities are being integrated into the activities of the associated workers; the capitalist division of labor separates these activities. This integration signifies that the conception of new techniques or new work processes no longer falls within the competence of a minority of specialists alone, but can be mastered by the great majority of workers, whose capabilities can thereby be fully mobilized.

We are witnessing the emergence of new social organizational forms of scientific and technical research. They involve reliance on what the Chinese call the mass line. It is indeed increasingly the masses themselves who are initiating and fostering technical change. The mass line has played, and continues to play, a basic role in the political struggles directed by the Chinese Communist Party. Today it also plays an essential role in the struggle for production and in the struggle for the collective mastery of science and technique by the workers. This has vast historical implications. If the term revolution has any meaning at all, it probably constitutes the true scientific and technical revolution of our time. The comprehensive results obtained thus far show clearly that this revolution is one part of the liberation of the productive forces made possible by socialism.

Socialist Development of the Productive Forces

The transformation of the conditions for the development of the productive forces currently being carried out in China is giving rise to a new kind of technical progress which is no longer limited and conditioned by capital—a fact, incidentally, that gives an utterly fanciful character to the attempts by economists to describe China in terms of the "models of development" they have constructed for the capitalist countries. This new type of technical progress corresponds to the socialist development of the productive forces.

What is most striking in the development of the productive forces in China is the fact that it is no longer closely subordinated to prior accumulation, precisely because it is based on a process of mass innovations and renovations. In the capitalist mode of production, technical transformations are very closely conditioned and dominated by a prior accumulation of capital, a result of the domination of dead labor over living labor. In socialist development of the productive forces this same accumulation, while still necessary, tends to play a secondary role with respect to the overall activity of the workers who constantly modify the means of production.

In visiting Chinese factories, one notices that production growth is no longer closely dependent on the amount of investment; thus, as Marx had anticipated, in socialist development of the productive forces it is living labor which is the directly and immediately decisive and dominant factor, whereas dead labor is but a subordinated and secondary factor. This affects the forms of the social division in production, as well as the relations between the production units and between the branches of industry. Although the division between one department (means of production) and another (consumer goods) of the economy is maintained under socialist conditions, its substance has been profoundly modified. The role of the first is no longer exclusively or predominantly to produce new machines; it gives diversified, direct and constant assistance to the aggregate production units with a view to enabling them to transform their own means of production.

The transformation of the manner of development of the productive forces is related to a number of other changes currently under way in China. An instance is the extremely rapid development of small and medium-sized enterprises. This development, which is occurring on a broad scale and is having a considerable economic impact, also testifies to the fact that the development of the productive forces is no longer heavily dominated by the prior accumulation of means of production.

One of the most striking aspects of the development of small enterprises is the emergence in the cities of "housewives' factories." These production units are generally initiated through the sole efforts and labor of housewives. Similar small production units have been established by people's communes and production brigades. This process should not be viewed as resulting merely from a momentary choice, but as occurring in the context of a new type of social organization—of new relations of production.

Most visitors to China in recent years have been struck by

the extraordinary proliferation of small and medium-sized enterprises. These enterprises have literally mushroomed. They have various juridical forms. Some are regarded as collective property—the small factories established by the production brigades and people's communes, or the street workshops initiated by city or suburban housewives. Others, such as the small factories established at the district level, fall into the category of state property. The development of new techniques no longer bound to the conditions of extended capitalist reproduction, to the accumulation and centralization of capital, has a direct effect on the multiplication of small and medium-sized enterprises.

In the capitalist mode of production, technical development is imprinted with the characteristic form of centralized capital; scientific and technical research is concentrated in technical processes that maximize the returns for strongly centralized capital; hence the continual increase in what under capitalist conditions constitutes the so-called optimal size of enterprises, as exemplified by the increasing size of steelworks, refineries, chemical plants, etc., which characterizes present-day capitalism.

In China, where the laws of extended capitalist reproduction are in the process of being shattered, technical progress takes a different form. Small modern production units can be as efficient as, and even more efficient than, large ones; their costs may be lower, and they require less investment per unit of productive capacity. Noteworthy in this respect are the small nitrate fertilizer factories with a capacity of a few thousand tons which currently operate in a very large number of rural districts. These factories use small compressors which, because of their small size, can also be easily produced in rural factories.

This expansion of small and medium-sized enterprises evidently reflects a political orientation which could be translated into such comprehensive practice only because it was fully attuned to new relations of production and new productive forces. What strikes the observer is not only the *prolif-eration* of small and medium-sized enterprises, but their *vitality*, their ability to develop by relying on their own resources, to advance in a few years from minimal size, with sometimes no more than five or six workers, to a productive capacity requiring two or three hundred workers, and this, as a rule, without the benefit of state investments but through self-growth and a great deal of self-equipment. It should be noted that these enterprises sell their products at prices fixed by the state, so they do not maintain excessive profit margins.

A concrete examination of these enterprises shows that their development presents two basic features. First are the new social and political conditions for technical progress, examined earlier, which because of the liberation of workers' initiative make possible the organic growth of the small enterprises and the progressive transformation of their means of production. Second is the existence of *socialist cooperation* between enterprises—the assistance given to the small and medium-sized enterprises by the larger and older enterprises, by their workers and technicians. These workers and technicians also help the districts, the production brigades of the people's communes, and the housewives to establish and run small and medium-sized factories and street workshops.

It is these two features that made possible the orientation toward a new type of rural industry, "elementary industrial networks," initially impelled by existing industrial activity on the district level. Each district has established or is in the process of establishing such an industrial network, which, after initial assistance, relies on its own resources in seeking to supply the district's essential needs with respect to consumption and extended reproduction.

The main feature of this process of development is that each district relies primarily on its own resources in developing its capacity to equip and finance itself. This type of development is specifically socialist, for it is based on the collective initiative of the masses.

A visitor to China's districts today notices the very visible beginnings of a profound change in rural life. The districts, people's communes, and production brigades have established thousands of small and medium-sized enterprises that provide the villages with electricity, cast iron, steel, construction materials, various metals, wire, farm implements, cultivators, fertilizers, textiles, and various chemical and pharmaceutical products, as well as daily necessities. A few figures will illustrate the scope of one of these elementary industrial networks.

Take the district of Tchia-ting, near Shanghai. This district has nineteen communes and four brigades and a population of 450,000. Before Liberation it had no modern industry at all; there were a few oil extraction mills equipped with wooden presses, a napkin factory in which weaving was done by hand, and a flour mill that used millstones. At the end of 1956 the district had 140 factories with 7,500 workers and employees, and an output valued at 31 million yuan. In 1960, after the Great Leap Forward, it had 341 factories employing 12,500 workers and producing an output valued at 42 million yuan. In 1971 it had 731 enterprises employing 20,000 workers and producing an industrial output valued at 115 million yuan. In other words, the value of this district's industrial output increased almost fourfold in less than fifteen years. This is by no means an exceptional case.

The development of elementary industrial networks constitutes the beginning of a profound break in the age-long opposition between town and countryside (town=industry/countryside=agriculture). This opposition is beginning to wither away—one of the essential features of socialist construction. Marx stressed the fact that this opposition underlies a whole set of contradictions that are characteristic of market and class societies.

The withering away of this opposition in China is reflected in rural industrial development and in a related effort to develop industry in the cities without increasing their population, which involves a political effort intended to persuade the workers in the large industrial centers to move to the rural areas. The concentration of huge populations in very large cities, such as Shanghai—a legacy of imperialism—is regarded as an intolerable situation that must be remedied. The Shanghai schools, for instance, yearly graduate about 200,000 youths who request work outside the city; workshops and entire departments are moved; the decisions are made after collective discussion in the factories about who is to leave, etc.

Rural industrialization brings about important changes in the nature of productive activity in these areas. These changes are made possible by a reduction of basic investment in agriculture and by the development of agricultural mechanization and semi-mechanization. This makes available a labor force that can be employed in industrial activities. We are therefore witnessing the emergence of a new spatial distribution of the productive forces, which are ceasing to be clustered around increasingly large cities, as is the case in capitalist countries. In China industrialization is accompanied—undoubtedly for the first time in history—by a process of disurbanization, certainly in very large cities such as Shanghai, but also in some like Chenyang, where the movement from the cities to the countryside has involved hundreds of thousands of people. This does not mean that industry in these cities is being neglected—on the contrary; but it does mean that their industrial development rests on a stable or decreasing urban population, whereas rural or small-town industrialization is accompanied by population growth.

The rural industrial networks are relatively autonomous. Their tasks include providing agriculture with the necessary means of production, raising agricultural output, improving working conditions, etc. All these changes are quite noticeable; they result from a comprehensive transformation of the relations of production. They required and made possible an ideological revolutionization—the introduction of a new proletarian world outlook in the countryside. For the peasants, this means the end of their traditional perceived domination by the cities. They are becoming conscious of the possibility of transforming themselves collectively and altering their condition and this modifies village life itself.

The Great Leap Forward had already made an important contribution in fostering this ideological transformation by making the peasant masses conscious of their ability to master industrial production processes. Rural industrialization required comprehensive changes in the relations between the central planning agencies and the various regional units. The people's communes and production brigades were allowed wide latitude so as to enable them to take the needs of the peasant masses into account. Once a number of largely political guidelines had been established, the small factories of the people's communes were free to use their own initiative.

To ensure coordination and prevent contradictions from arising, politics must be put in command—that is, the regions and production units must give priority to overall interests. This requires each individual at the base to acquire a grasp of the nature of the general interest, and implies a new attitude on the part of the masses with respect to overall political and economic problems.

The policy of rural industrialization and decentralization is effective only because it rests on social relations and productive forces which enable it to become rooted in reality. This is the opposite of the "voluntarism" and "subjectivism" of which the Chinese leaders are so readily accused. These charges are utterly false. What is striking, on the contrary, is the extraordinary realism of a policy which excludes neither imagination nor bold initiatives.

4. Revolutionizing the Relations of Production

The historical experiences of the Soviet Union and China raise questions about the social consequences of different "methods of management," which correspond to the social conditions underlying the use of the means of production and the allocation of tasks. Depending on the social form of management, those who determine the use made of the means of production, the allocation of tasks, and the nature of production constitute either a minority standing apart from material production or a majority—the immediate producers. We are therefore dealing here with production relations and class relationships.

The production relations that are reproduced in a factory, however, basically reflect the social relationships that are reproduced in the social formation as a whole, and the class struggle being waged throughout the society. The socialist transformation of the production relations always results from class struggle and, above all, from the ideological and political class struggle being waged throughout the social formation.

In the combination productive forces/production relations, the latter play the dominant role by imposing the conditions under which the productive forces are reproduced. Conversely, the development of the productive forces never directly determines the transformation of the production relations; this transformation is always the focus of intervention by the contending classes—that is, of class struggle.

The struggle for the socialist transformation of the production relations cannot be waged in the name of the "development of the productive forces," since the forms this development assumes reflect class relationships and are determined by the class interests, perceptions, aspirations, and ideas of the contending classes. Marx stressed this point on more than one occasion, particularly when he pointed out that a distinction should always be made between change in the economic base and upheaval in the superstructure and added that it is through the legal and political superstructure, "to which correspond definite forms of social consciousness," that people engage in struggle and fight it out.[1]

Since the transformation of the production relations is a function of the class struggle, it follows that even when the bourgeoisie has lost political power capitalist production relations can continue to reproduce themselves, for they are conditioned by a production process which does not undergo an immediate transformation. Before a new system of social relationships can be fully developed and a new mode of production fully instituted, the social formation necessarily passes through a period of transition. During this period social relationships must be completely revolutionized.

The novelty and complexity of socialism, which is a transition from capitalism to communism, derive from its very nature—it is a historically unprecedented passage from a class society to a classless society. During the socialist transition the new production relations are not yet fully dominant; according to an expression frequently used in China, they are still "imperfect." They are communist production relations in an embryonic stage, and their development clashes with the existing market relations and capitalist relations.

The inevitable character of this "imperfection" was under-

1. See Karl Marx, Preface to *A Contribution to the Critique of Political Economy.*

lined by Marx when he declared that the socialist society is "in every respect, economically, morally and intellectually, still stamped with the birthmarks of the old society from whose womb it emerges." Mao Tse-tung emphasized this idea on a number of occasions, notably when he stated in 1957:

> The new social system has only just been established and requires time for its consolidation. It must not be assumed that the new system can be completely consolidated the moment it is established, for that is impossible. It has to be consolidated step by step. To achieve its ultimate consolidation, it is necessary not only to bring about the socialist industrialization of the country and persevere in the socialist revolution on the economic front, but to carry on constant and arduous socialist revolutionary struggles and socialist education on the political and ideological fronts. Moreover, various contributory international factors are required. [2]

The incomplete or imperfect development of the socialist production relations is paralleled by the partial reproduction, even under the dictatorship of the proletariat, of the old production relations; these disappear—or they can be destroyed—only insofar as they are completely replaced by socialist relations. Lenin clearly indicated this characteristic of socialism:

> Theoretically, there can be no doubt that between capitalism and communism there lies a definite transition period which must combine the features and properties of both these forms of social economy. This transition period has to be a period of struggle between dying capitalism and nascent communism—or, in other words, between capitalism which has been defeated but not destroyed and communism which has been born but is still very feeble. [3]

2. "Speech at the Chinese Communist Party's National Conference on Propaganda Work" (March 12, 1957), in *Quotations from Chairman Mao Tse-tung* (Peking: Foreign Languages Press, 1966), pp. 27-28.

3. Lenin, "Economics and Politics in the Era of the Dictatorship of the Proletariat," in *Selected Works,* vol. 3 (Moscow: Progress Publishers, 1967), p. 274.

The "imperfect" character of socialism, which is a transition between the capitalist and communist modes of production, constitutes one of the objective bases of the struggle between the two roads.

This question gave rise to a good deal of confusion in the U.S.S.R. in the thirties, where it was considered that the construction of socialism had been "completed." Accordingly, socialism was no longer conceived as a transition, but as a stabilized mode of production whose eventual transformation did not appear to be related to class struggle but was dependent on a process of extended reproduction of the existing relations.[4] During the socialist transition, however, classes continue to exist and the transformation of the social process of production continues to be conditioned by the class struggle, and primarily by the ideological class struggle—capitalist social relations must be destroyed. To this end, the surviving capitalist relations must first be relegated to a subordinate place at all levels of the social formation.

The displacement of the principal aspect of the contradiction between capitalist social relations and communist social relations proceeds unevenly. The institution of the dictatorship of the proletariat displaces the principal aspect of the contradiction in favor of the proletariat on the *political* level, and partially on the ideological level; but in a first stage, as long as the proletariat is not in control of every production unit, this displacement does not occur, or occurs only very partially, in the economic base itself, at the level of production relations. The partial reproduction of the old production relations, which manifests itself notably in the form of capitalist "management" of the industrial enterprises, constitutes one of the objective bases of the existence of the bourgeoisie.

The ideological and political class struggle which continues

4. See the *Handbook of Political Economy* of the Academy of Sciences of the U.S.S.R., and Stalin's writings of 1936.

throughout the transition rests both on this objective basis and on the reproduction, through the ideological and political apparatuses, of bourgeois social relationships. Only an ideological and political proletarian struggle can destroy the old capitalist social relations, including production relations, and fully develop socialist production relations. Progress along the road to socialism depends on the struggle of the proletariat and is never the direct result of a "development of the productive forces" alone. This is why the transition passes through stages characterized by ideological and political struggle. This struggle determines the direction of every social formation moving toward socialism.

The manner in which the class struggle develops under the dictatorship of the proletariat depends primarily on the political line of the ruling party. This line represents an approximate concentration of the correct ideas of the masses, which enables them to draw the lessons of their own experience and that of past proletarian struggles. The political line also constitutes the chief factor making it possible to reject capitalist forms of management. The transformation of industrial management is quite different from a mere modification of "management techniques." It focuses on the production relations themselves, which can be revolutionized only through class struggle. When the proletariat has the initiative, this struggle leads through successive stages to the appropriation by the masses of proletarian ideology and to the effective social appropriation of the means of production.

In the social formations in which it develops, the capitalist mode of production brings about a transformation of the work process. One of the aspects of this transformation is the use of machines, which brings into being the collective worker. The former individual relationship of the worker to his work tool disintegrates, and the workers integrated into and dominated by capitalist production relations face the machines collectively, while divided hierarchically and organized in separate production units.

The concept of "collective worker" must be distinguished from that of "associated worker," which designates what Marx calls the "freely associated" workers who enter into relationships differing fundamentally from those that keep them in subjection to capital. This is where the elimination of the bourgeois division of labor intervenes, for the existence of the fully developed associated worker presupposes the end of the division between manual labor and intellectual labor, between administrative tasks and performance tasks, between town and countryside, and between organizationally separated "production units." The Cultural Revolution marks the beginning of the destruction of the old collective worker and the birth of the associated worker—the birth of socially unified work.

In order for the means of production to be socially appropriated—that is, in order for the immediate producers to exercise effective collective control over the means of production—the working class must overcome its division and achieve unity, and the unity of the immediate producers and their means of production must prevail over their separation.

So long as a sufficient degree of unity has not been attained, the immediate producers cannot exercise direct social control on a broad scale. They can exercise control only through the intermediary of the ruling proletarian party, which is the instrument of the ideological and political unity of the working class and the broad masses and which is therefore essential to the dictatorship of the proletariat. This party can be the instrument of the dictatorship of the proletariat only if it is the carrier of proletarian ideology, and if it ensures the gradual appropriation by the masses of this ideology through a social practice which requires that the relationship between the party and the masses remain an internal rather than an external one.

The fact that the working class and the broad masses support the activities of the proletarian party, however, does not necessarily mean that the masses have already appropriated

proletarian ideology and that their practice is no longer dominated by bourgeois ideology, especially with respect to the
struggle for production. As long as this bourgeois ideology
has not been overcome, the working class and the broad
masses remain divided and can be induced to give priority to
partial or individual interests at the expense of the overall
interests of the revolution. This was to a certain extent the
situation in People's China during the years following Liberation, and explains what Mao Tse-tung wrote at that time: "In
our economic and financial set-up, we must overcome such
evils as disunity, assertion of independence and lack of coordination, and must establish a working system which is unified and responsive to direction and which permits the full
application of our policies and regulations."[5]

The Cultural Revolution enabled the workers to take an
important step toward their appropriation of proletarian
ideology and created the conditions for the achievement of
unified mass action. The Chinese Communist Party's political
line thus made it possible to achieve an unprecedented unity
of viewpoints, political measures, plans, directives, and
actions. Accordingly, every enterprise now considers, much
more readily than before, the overall interests of the country
rather than its own.

Ideological revolutionization—the growing appropriation
by the masses of proletarian ideology—is one of the necessary
conditions for the revolutionization of production relations,
precisely because socialist development requires the social
appropriation of the means of production; this necessitates a
collective process during which nature and the productive
forces are appropriated—it requires true collective action. In
order for such a social collective process of appropriation to
develop fully, the immediate producers must be effectively
united in action and concept and with respect to ends and
means. This unity cannot be imposed from without; it is of

5. Quoted in *Peking Review*, April 17, 1970, p. 9.

necessity a unity of practice, ideas, and perceptions—a political and ideological unity which requires that individual or particular interests be subordinated to collective interests. As long as this is not the case, the social appropriation of the means of production and of output remains imperfect, that is, partially formal.

Engels stressed this fact when he declared that state ownership of the means of production is but a formal means of resolving the contradiction between the social character of the productive forces and the private character of appropriation. State ownership of the means of production—even when the state constitutes the dictatorship of the proletariat—is not yet real social appropriation; it designates a legal relationship and not an overall transformation of production relations.

As Engels pointed out, in taking possession of the means of production the state appropriates them "in the name of society," which clearly means that this is not as yet a social appropriation (an appropriation by "society" itself). It also means that the immediate producers have not yet appropriated the means of production directly and collectively. The state, in fact, exists only in terms of its separation from the immediate producers. This is why the state must cease to exist before the complete unity of the means of production and the immediate producers can be realized. This, of course, requires a long historical process.

The abolition of private legal ownership of the means of production and the institution of an economic plan are necessary but insufficient conditions for the effective social appropriation of the means of production. Such an appropriation requires a radical transformation of the social production process, which cannot be forced upon the immediate producers but must result from unified collective action. This unity is in turn possible only if the broad masses reject the nonproletarian ideologies which divide them and make possible the reproduction of exploitative relations.

The Cultural Revolution represents a form of class struggle that enables the masses to appropriate proletarian ideology, but it is only a stage in a more extensive appropriation process that corresponds to an objective requirement of socialist construction. As long as this requirement is not satisfied, or is satisfied only partially, concepts deriving from the ideology of the exploiting class continue to exist. These concepts make it possible to divide the workers and subject them to exploitative relations. They also make possible the reproduction of these relations and the private appropriation by an exploiting class of the means of production and output. This possibility subsists whatever the *juridical form* assumed by private appropriation—it may be that of "state ownership" or "collective ownership" and may even include those forms which *best dissimulate* the exploitative relations, since they represent private appropriation under the guise of its opposite.

The appropriation by the masses of proletarian ideology is essential insofar as this ideology enables the masses to unify themselves by initiating an analysis of the contradictions, and thus to resolve these contradictions through class struggle. The appropriation by the immediate producers of proletarian ideology enables them to comprehend that the social process of production is not simply a "juxtaposition" of "individual acts," but a collective activity which must be dealt with as such before it can be brought under control. As long as the social process of production cannot be dealt with as a single process by the immediate producers, it is divided into more or less separate elementary processes. The unity of the social process is then maintained through the intervention of agents who are extraneous to production and who, unless subjected to the political leadership of the proletariat expressed in a proletarian dictatorship, constitute a dominant and exploiting class.

Since the relations through which the unity of the production process is realized appear as "necessary," the ideology of the class which dominates the social process of production represents this process as a simple sum of individual or particular processes which can be realized, coordinated, and "perfected" only through the intervention of privileged agents placed above the immediate producers. Both bourgeois ideology and that of the other exploiting classes thus provide an illusory "justification" for modes of production that imply a basic social division—the division into classes. By creating the illusion that the exploited can "liberate" themselves individually or through isolated actions, this ideology fosters division within the dominated class itself, enabling the dominant class to maintain exploitation and reproduce the social and material conditions essential to exploitation.

And again, if proletarian politics is not in command in the management of the enterprises, the enterprises are divided among themselves in the same way that the immediate producers are divided among themselves. The dominant factor will then be either market and money relations or a production plan imposed upon the immediate producers from without. In the first case, it is profit which is in command; in the second, production. In both instances, the activity of the immediate producers is in fact subordinated to particular interests and not to the overall interests of the revolution.

When proletarian politics is not in command, each enterprise tends to promote its own interests rather than the overall interest, whether to make more profit or to realize its "plan." Instead of effectively cooperating among themselves and eventually carrying out more difficult or less "profitable" tasks, the enterprises do their utmost to secure the easiest plan or the most profitable orders. There is much scheming to obtain specific orders and plans, to secure more production facilities, or to have goods of poor quality certified as acceptable. At the same time, the workers, instead of applying themselves to revolutionizing the production relations, are urged to produce a maximum output in the name of their personal interest, individual incentives play a decisive role, and the entire incentive system demands supervision, control, and a hierarchical organization which ensures the reproduction of capitalist relations in the enterprises while causing proletarian ideology to wane. Money is then the dominant factor in production as well as in the plan itself.

Under such conditions the initiative and enthusiasm of the masses are stifled and production can increase only through the accumulation of additional means of production and through technical changes instigated from the top. Accumulation—the driving force of capitalist extended reproduction—comes to prevail over the socialist development of the productive forces. The central role of accumulation determines the specific content of the economic plan—an overriding concern with the need to produce an output that exceeds the consumption of the masses, with the result that the needs of the masses are neglected. This in turn undermines the initiative of the immediate producers and their will to work. Under these conditions the producers must be made to achieve the plan's objectives through a system of individual material reward and repression. Such a system enables a class that is extraneous to the immediate producers to reestablish or extend its control over the workers and consequently to exploit them.

It must be emphasized that, contrary to the assertions of revisionist ideology, the concern with profit cannot produce results "analagous" to those obtained when proletarian politics is put in the forefront. Ideologically, a preoccupation with profit and the primacy of individual and particular interests are incompatible with proletarian ideology. Politically, the predominance of individual interest is bound to strengthen controls, distrust, and repression. Economically, there is always a contradiction between particular interests and the overall interests of the workers and of the revolution.

It is an "economist" illusion, analogous to that of "liberalism," to believe that a "system" is possible which can create complete harmony between a preoccupation with individual interest and the need to satisfy the overall interest. There are constantly cases when what is most "satisfactory" to a particular enterprise is not satisfactory to the workers as a whole, or in terms of the revolutionization of the production relations, or to the world revolution. There are constantly cases when the need to satisfy the general interest requires individuals or enterprises to make sacrifices. As the Chinese put it, "We must not forget that we ourselves and our enterprise are but part of a whole, and that in carrying out our individual work we must always try to take the whole into consideration."

In giving priority to proletarian politics the Chinese workers are transforming the enterprises, which have now ceased to be mere "production units" and are becoming interrelated political units, in which the producers are exercising their power, and ideological units. In this connection, Mao Tse-tung has stated that when priority is given to proletarian politics, "management is also socialist education."[6] Putting proletarian politics in command is therefore essential to socialist management of the enterprises, to the development of socialist productive forces, to the growth of the will to struggle, and to the socialist transformation of the producers.

The Cultural Revolution represents a very important and unprecedented stage along the road of socialist development, but it is no more than a stage. The class struggle is far from finished and the struggle between the two lines continues. Accordingly, criticism and campaigns to rectify the work style of the new organizations are constantly necessary. Without such criticism and campaigns there is the inevitable risk that these organizations may move away from the socialist road. In August 1967, Mao Tse-tung stressed his belief that several cultural revolutions will be necessary:

6. *Peking Review,* April 17, 1970, p. 10.

The present Great Cultural Revolution is only the first of its kind. There will of necessity be several of these revolutions in the future. The question of which will win out, socialism or capitalism, requires a very long historical period before it can be settled. If the struggle is not waged successfully, the restoration of capitalism will remain a constant possibility.

Postscript

On rereading the preceding pages, I find that they throw insufficient light on the fact that the transformations in the social relationships brought about by the Cultural Revolution did not result from "spontaneous" mass action inspired by the illusory views of the "ideology of spontaneity," but from mass action aided by the political guidelines of Mao Tse-tung's revolutionary line, and from the activities of the workers, peasants, cadres, etc., who adhered to this line. These guidelines and activities alone made it possible to concentrate the correct initiatives of the workers, and enabled the Chinese masses to unify their struggles and to define the objectives they had to attain before they could hope to overcome a bourgeois line and social relationships that obstruct China's progress along the road to socialism.

Insofar as I did not adequately elucidate the active role of the revolutionary line and failed to provide sufficient historical data regarding the conditions under which it challenged the bourgeois line, the wrong impression may have been created that the social transformations in question were the "assured" outcome of favorable objective conditions alone. Such a view would obscure the scope and complexity of the struggles which the Chinese masses had to wage against the bourgeois line, under both its revisionist and "ultra-leftist" guises.

To gain a better understanding of the struggles that occurred during the Cultural Revolution it should be kept in mind that although the çontradictions which the Cultural Revolution made it possible to resolve—thus helping China to advance along the road to socialism—were indeed objective conditions, the Cultural Revolution nevertheless became an effective force only because the masses had been summoned to action by the Central Committee of the Chinese Communist Party (notably through the decision of the Central Committee, "Concerning the Great Proletarian Cultural Revolution," adopted on August 8, 1966, and through the communiqué of the Eleventh Plenary Session of the Central Committee, adopted on August 12, 1966), and it came to have a profound impact only insofar as the Chinese masses appropriated the revolutionary ideas of Marxism. It should also be recalled that the implementation of the revolutionary line was impeded by the presence of bourgeois and petty-bourgeois ideas among the masses themselves. If these ideas had not been prevalent among the masses, the bourgeois line could have mobilized only the handful of people who stood to gain from its victory.

The Cultural Revolution, therefore, should be viewed as a stage in the struggle between the proletarian line of the Chinese Communist Party and the bourgeois line. This stage has its particular characteristics, to be sure; but the struggle itself continues—it existed before the Cultural Revolution and is destined to continue as long as the bourgeoisie and bourgeois ideas continue to exist, and as long as the bourgeoisie and the proletariat continue to confront each other. These points will become clearer if a number of crucial considerations are kept in mind.

If proletariat and bourgeoisie continue to exist under the dictatorship of the proletariat, this is because capitalist relations (which are the objective foundation of both bourgeoisie and proletariat) do not simply vanish when the proletarian revolution occurs, or even when socialist forms of ownership come to prevail. Because of the continued existence of these capitalist relations, the workers continue to be partially separated from the means of production and a minority retains the possibility of determining the employment of the means of production. The basic objective of the proletarian line is precisely to destroy both capitalist relations and the classes based on these relations. This objective can be attained only through the revolutionary transformation of social relations as a whole—political and ideological as well as production relations.

The basic objective of the bourgeois line is to maintain class divisions through the preservation and, if possible, development of capitalist relations. The activities inspired by the bourgeois line pursue this objective regardless of what the adherents of this line, especially ordinary workers, "think" this objective represents. And because of the very nature of the class relations and of the class struggle determined by these relations, the bourgeois line presents itself in two seemingly contradictory aspects.

One aspect has a rather obvious conservative character. Its adherents advocate "postponing" all new changes in the social relations until "the productive forces are sufficiently developed"; in the meantime they proclaim the need for "economic efficiency," which in turn is said to require a special kind of discipline. In China, this aspect of the bourgeois line corresponded to Liu Shao-chi's line. Since it has been frequently analyzed, among others by Jean Daubier in *Histoire de la révolution culturelle prolétarienne en Chine,* which I have already cited, I will not dwell on this point.

The other aspect of the bourgeois line presents itself under the guise of its "opposite," with the result that its conservative character is obscured and only a careful analysis of its slogans and practices can elucidate its true class character. This second aspect of the bourgeois line corresponds to the "ultra-leftist" line and was very widespread during the Cultural Revolution. This postscript is intended primarily to provide some particulars and to present a few facts and reflections concerning the activities of the proponents of this line, which have given rise to a great deal of confusion.

The ultra-leftist line advanced two kinds of slogans. On the one hand, it pushed measures that did not correspond to the needs and possibilities of the moment, thus trying to represent a secondary contradiction as a principal contradiction and dividing the workers by presenting them with objectives that cannot be realized at the moment. On the other hand—and this was more important—it launched petty-bourgeois slogans—slogans corresponding to the guise which bourgeois ideology assumes when it is operative among the masses. These slogans obstruct viable transformations by presenting the masses with objectives that appear "radical" but do not lead in the direction of a real transformation of social relationships. In the long run these slogans tend to disarm, discourage, and divide the masses. Ultra-leftist activity undermined the revolutionary unity of the masses with respect to many other questions as well; for instance, it tried to force some people's communes to abandon the practice of making payment reflect the amount of work done, or immediately and completely to give up private individual plots of land and farming, before they were ready for this.

In order to understand how the bourgeois line manifested itself under its ultra-leftist guise during the Cultural Revolution, we must briefly recall some of the measures and forms of action advanced by this line, so that they may be compared with the slogans and activities of the proletarian line.

Whereas the proletarian line waged an ideological class struggle designed to enable the masses to appropriate the ideas and analyses of Marxism-Leninism, and those who were the targets of criticism to understand their errors and rectify them, the ultra-left resorted whenever possible to personal attacks, humiliation sessions, and even physical violence. On

July 29, 1967, I witnessed such a humiliation session at the Shanghai Iron and Steel Institute. I thought at the time that this represented an isolated case without wider political implications. When I visited this Institute again in 1971, I learned that these humiliation sessions had been initiated by adherents of the ultra-left, that they had been numerous, and that they had eventually resulted in the use of physical violence. Work at the Institute was paralyzed for months and resumed only after the leading member of the ultra-left at the Institute had been expelled; the person in question, incidentally, was not a worker but an intellectual.

Under the conditions then prevailing in China, the substitution of personal attacks, humiliation sessions, and violence for ideological class struggle was characteristic of a bourgeois line. Whereas the criticism of false ideas helps the masses to gain increasing understanding of what is correct and what false—of what corresponds to the interests of the revolution and to their own—personal attacks cannot possibly achieve this essential end. Rather than helping their targets to rectify errors, these attacks discourage rectification, especially when they represent simple administrative mistakes, or even acts in no way to be faulted, as grave political errors.[1]

Above all, personal attacks tend to direct the attention of the masses to facts that are not essential, such as a person's past, and divert their attention from what is essential—false and correct ideas and their origins, the social relationships and social practices in which these ideas are rooted and which must be transformed. In launching personal attacks the ultra-left made extensive use of the "biographical" method, which consisted in accumulating particulars concerning every party member's life history. This diverted the attention of the masses from the analysis of ideas and easily observable prac-

1. The periodical *Vento dell'Est*, no. 26, provides many particulars regarding the activities of the ultra-leftists and their consequences in the factories as well as in the universities. See pp. 35ff. concerning activities in the universities.

tices, and tried to undermine their efforts at analysis by getting them to wait passively for the "revelations" supposedly contained in "secret documents."

The substitution of personal attacks for ideological class struggle corresponds to a bourgeois and petty-bourgeois practice and therefore pursues specific political ends. In resorting to these practices the ultra-left sought to achieve two complementary ends: the replacement of experienced and dedicated revolutionary cadres with its own people; and the preservation of existing social relationships. It accordingly advanced the notion that it is more important to replace one person with another than to revolutionize prevailing social relationships. During 1967 the ultra-left openly advocated a "life-and-death struggle" in the style of "dragging out Peng into broad daylight" and "beating the dog in the water."[2] This shows clearly that the ultra-left was concerned not with transforming social relationships but with personalizing ongoing struggles.

During the latter half of 1967 the proponents of the revolutionary line increasingly insisted on the need to wage a twofold campaign—first, to "completely discredit the handful of party persons in authority taking the capitalist road," and second, to "carry to success the struggle-criticism-transformation in the respective units,"[3] in other words, to struggle for the transformation of social relationships. The ultra-left, for its part, continued to speak only of criticisms and condemnations, which enabled it to ignore the task of revolutionizing the social relationships.[4]

During my visit to the Shanghai Iron and Steel Institute, a member of the revolutionary committee, whom I questioned

2. *Peking Review*, no. 35 (August 25, 1967), p. 7.

3. *Peking Review*, no. 43 (October 20, 1967), p. 10.

4. This orientation of the ultra-leftist line was still being disseminated in 1968, as in an article published in China and translated in *Peking Review*, no. 37 (September 13, 1968), p. 4, which deals essentially with "fierce attacks," "relentless" struggles, and the need to "uncover all the counter-revolutionaries who are hiding in dark corners," and not with transforming social relationships.

about the ultra-left, made the following reply: "Instead of struggle-criticism-transformation [the ultra-leftists] want only struggle-criticism; they want to abandon the Institute instead of transforming it. They want to abandon the old intellectuals instead of helping them to transform their bourgeois ideas. The ultra-leftists do not understand that one divides into two, and that old intellectuals also have knowledge that may be useful to socialism. We struggle against these mistaken tendencies."[5]

The orientations deriving from Mao Tse-tung's proletarian line conform to the Chinese Communist Party's long-standing revolutionary practice and have an altogether different character. They pose the problem of "transformation"—of the need to transform social relationships and the management of industrial production units (in keeping with the principles of the Anshan Constitution), and to reeducate both cadres who have made errors and intellectuals. In September 1968 the following directive by Mao Tse-tung was published:

> Here we wish to raise the question of giving attention to re-educating the large numbers of college and secondary school graduates who started work quite some time ago as well as those who have just begun to work, so that they will integrate with the workers and peasants. Some of them are sure to make a success of this integration and achieve something in regard to inventions and innovations. Mention should be made of these people as encouragement. Those who are really impossible, that is, the diehard capitalist roaders and bourgeois technical authorities who have incurred the extreme wrath of the masses and therefore must be overthrown, are very few in number. Even they should be given a

5. During a conversation on September 7, 1971, in the course of my trip to China, it was stated that the ultra-left distorted the struggle against "tailism" and subservience to things foreign by asserting that it was useless to read foreign periodicals and books. The revolutionary line, on the other hand, holds that it is necessary "critically to assimilate the old and foreign so as to make it serve the new and Chinese." The ultra-leftist campaign against the study of foreign experiences was in fact inspired by chauvinist tendencies that are characteristic of the bourgeoisie and petty bourgeoisie.

way out. To do otherwise is not the policy of the proletariat. The above-mentioned policies should be applied to both new and old intellectuals, whether working in the arts or sciences.[6]

Two opposed lines are apparent here—a bourgeois line under its ultra-leftist guise, which resorts to personal attacks and "life-and-death" struggles, and a proletarian line which stands for reeducation and the transformation of social relationships.

In substituting personal attacks for ideological class struggle, the ultra-left advances abstract moral criteria by which it "judges" individuals. One of these criteria is that of selfishness. The ultra-left constantly calls for abstract struggle against self-interest—what it sometimes calls "eradicating the thought of self." Such a struggle is an illusory substitute for the eradication of bourgeois social relationships and for effective struggle against revisionism. An article published in China in 1967 contains the following:

> [S]elf-interest is the core of the bourgeois world outlook and the hotbed of revisionism. Revisionism is the inevitable outcome of the development of self-interest. If self-interest is not knocked down, the theories, line, principles and policies as put forward by Chairman Mao concerning the great proletarian cultural revolution cannot be really understood and implemented, the general orientation of struggle cannot be grasped well and the anti-revisionist struggle cannot be carried through to the end ... the socialist motherland cannot be safeguarded unless self-interest is overcome and concern for public interest reigns.[7]

Such assertions obscure the real nature of revisionism: it is a bourgeois political line deeply rooted in the existence of the bourgeoisie and its underlying social relationships. For the ultra-left, revisionism and capitalism are simply "products" of self-interest. This view reflects a bourgeois world outlook and idealist concepts. It has nothing in common with historical

6. *Peking Review*, no. 37 (September 13, 1968), p. 13.
7. *Peking Review*, no. 42 (October 13, 1967), p. 16.

materialism and Marxism, where ideas, whether correct or false, "do not fall from the sky," but derive from practice and always have a class character.

To be sure, it is not under the simplistic guise of ideas that "fall from the sky" that the ultra-left could permit itself to advance its idealist concepts. It does not represent self-interest as a "natural human trait," as does traditional bourgeois idealism, but as a remnant of capitalism supposedly surviving only "in people's minds." A 1967 *Hongqi* editorial stated:

> The core of the system of ideas of the exploiting classes is egoism, selfishness. As a result of the thousands of years of existence of the system of private ownership, such egoism has a deep-rooted influence. The old social system has been eliminated, but as our great leader Chairman Mao has observed, "Invariably, remnants of old ideas reflecting the old system remain in people's minds for a long time, and they do not easily give way." The bourgeoisie makes use of precisely this trash to corrupt the masses and the younger generation, to try to conquer the hearts of the people, and to fight against the proletariat.[8]

The unqualified assertion that "the old social system has been eliminated" implies that classes and their ideology *can no longer have any roots in the present;* this makes the ideological remnants themselves incomprehensible, and, above all, sets only a "moral target" for the masses and not a political target as well—the destruction of the social relationships that underlie the existence, practices, and ideas of the bourgeoisie. Consequently, the assertion that the *only* ideas that survive were produced by bourgeois relations which have already been eliminated leaves the bourgeois relations themselves intact. This view is identical with that of Liu Shao-chi, who also singled out the task of "hunting down" mistaken ideas.

The ultra-left not only helps maintain the persisting bourgeois relations by denying that they exist, but also obstructs

8. Translated in ibid., p. 11.

the struggle against selfishness. Such a struggle is necessary in that it is an essential stage in an ideological struggle the aim of which is not the illusory immediate and total destruction of selfishness, but the *concrete* confrontation of this quality within the framework of an ideological revolution that clears the way for economic, material transformations which alone can make it possible to consolidate the proletarian ideology. The materialist view of history clearly shows that progress in the direction of a classless society requires the continuous transformation of the objective relations and of ideology through successive stages of offensive and consolidation. In advancing abstract and idealist slogans, the ultra-left actually implements a bourgeois line under a "leftist" guise.

It may be useful to compare the ultra-leftist and revolutionary positions with respect to this question. The views of the revolutionary line are stated with great clarity in a recent article in *Hongqi* entitled "Why Is It Necessary to Study Political Economy?" The article contains the following passage:

> In socialist society, the production relations and the productive forces, as well as the superstructure and the economic base, are at one and the same time in accord (this is the basic feature) and in contradiction. The socialist relations of production correspond to the development of the productive forces, but they are not yet perfect, and this imperfection is in contradiction with the development of the productive forces. The socialist superstructure corresponds to the economic base, but it still contains insufficiencies that are in contradiction with the socialist economic base. In particular, the capitalist factors in the relations of production and in the domain of the superstructure impede the development of the productive forces, weaken and even undermine the socialist economic base. The proletariat and other laboring masses desirous of taking the socialist road always demand the continuous transformation of those aspects of the production relations and the superstructure that do not correspond, respectively, to the productive forces and the economic base, so that the socialist relations of production and the socialist super-

structure may be constantly strengthened and improved. The bourgeoisie and its agents in the party who want to take the capitalist road are always trying to obstruct this transformation. The reason for this is that such a transformation gradually eliminates the capitalist factors in the relations of production and the superstructure, and that the elimination of the capitalist factors signifies the elimination of the bourgeoisie and its agents within the party.[9]

It is clear that for the revolutionary line an essential aspect of "the elimination of the bourgeoisie and its agents within the party" is the revolutionary transformation of the social relationships.

The petty-bourgeois character of the ultra-leftist line was particularly evident in its approach to the question of factory work regulation. In this context, too, there is a sharp contrast between the views based on the revolutionary line and those advocated by the "ultra-left." The adherents of the revolutionary line were concerned with the elimination of what the Chinese call "unreasonable rules"—the "codification" of work regulations (previously enforced by factory managers influenced by revisionism) which "protected" bourgeois production relations and capitalist forms of the division of labor in the industrial enterprises. These included the separation between manual labor and intellectual labor, between performance tasks and administrative tasks, and the subordination of the immediate producers to technicians, engineers, administrators, managers, etc.[10] For the proponents of the revolutionary line the elimination of "unreasonable rules" was to enable the working class to institute revolutionary work regulations and unite technicians, engineers, and cadres under its leadership. In practice, the ultra-left posed the question of work regulation in altogether different terms. What it

9. Agence Chine Nouvelle, September 1, 1972, bulletin no. 1496, dispatch no. 083107.

10. See *Vento dell'Est*, no. 26, especially p. 26 and pp. 35ff., for information on this and other aspects of the "ultra-left."

advocated was not the concrete transformation of work regulations—the transformation of the codified forms of the production relations and division of labor—but the illusory elimination of any regulation whatever with respect to work safety, attendance, quality control, etc.

In making this demand the ultra-left pursued several objectives. In proposing an unattainable goal—the elimination of all rules—rather than a realistic goal—the effective socialist transformation of the social relations and of the rules by which they are "codified"—the ultra-left in fact obstructed the attainment of the viable goal. Furthermore, by opposing the socialist transformation of the division of labor and indefinitely prolonging a struggle pursuing an illusory goal, it helped disorganize production and violate the slogan "grasp revolution, promote production," and tended to discredit the Cultural Revolution in the eyes of the masses, who were getting weary of endless discussions and confrontations and of their destructive effects on production and everyday life. The ultra-left mobilized mass dissatisfaction with bourgeois work regulations and at the same time *diverted* it by encouraging its petty-bourgeois rather than proletarian aspects. It did this in various ways, but principally by legitimizing "private" discontent and sanctioning the view that individuals should not work unless they feel like it. Such a notion, of course, has nothing in common with communism—it reflects the distorted ideas of "communism" as it is construed by the bourgeoisie and petty bourgeoisie.

Through its activities and slogans the ultra-left placed numerous obstacles in the path of victory for the revolutionary line. The masses and revolutionary cadres of the Chinese Communist Party overcame these obstacles because they were able to develop proletarian practices inspired by the revolutionary line and Mao Tse-tung's instructions. These instructions summed up the lessons to be drawn from both the creative initiatives of the masses and the destructive practices of the ultra-left; they gave concrete indications regarding the real goal to be pursued—the struggle against the capitalist division of labor—and the means to be used to that end—the elimination of "unreasonable rules," especially through the institution of three-in-one combinations under the leadership of the working class.

When the masses had appropriated these guidelines, particularly by fully assimilating the revolutionary content of the May 16 directive, they were able to overcome ultra-leftist opposition to the effective transformation of production relations. The ultra-left then suffered its first major defeat, but it retained some of the organizational influence it had gained by promoting the petty-bourgeois aspect of mass aspirations, an approach that had enabled it to disregard the revolutionary and proletarian aspect of these same mass aspirations.

The same opposition between the proletarian orientation of the revolutionary line and the petty-bourgeois orientation of the ultra-left was evident in regard to the question of wages. For the adherents of the proletarian line the basic task is the most thorough possible elimination of material incentives, for they strengthen the workers' (individualist) bourgeois relationships to their work. For the ultra-left, on the contrary, the basic task was the restructuring of the entire wage system.

Although the revolutionary line also poses the question of restructuring the wage system (a concern which led to decisive changes through the elimination of the material incentive denounced by the masses, the simplification of a complex wage structure which divided the workers, etc.), it does not view this as a basic and immediate problem. Proceeding from a Marxist viewpoint, it holds that, as Marx said, distribution relations are always "the reverse side of the production relations." This is precisely why the proletarian line stresses the crucial importance of revolutionizing the production rather than the distribution relations, for it is illusory to believe that the latter can be revolutionized as long as the production relations remain unchanged.

For the proletarian line, moreover, the goal of the revolution is communism, that is, the elimination of the wage system itself. The transition period must therefore prepare the way for the elimination of wage relations, not only by revolutionizing production relations, but by developing forms of distribution that provide compensation for existing inequalities (with respect to physical strength, health, etc.) by means other than wages. In fact, compensating these inequalities by means of wages tends to prolong the existence of the wage form; this is why it is preferable whenever possible to resort to compensations corresponding to collective forms of distribution and deriving from sources "outside" the wage relations; such is the case when canteens, day-care centers, health services, etc., are made increasingly available.

By its unqualified stress on egalitarianism in the area of wages, the ultra-left tended, in fact, to strengthen the wage form. It further evidenced the bourgeois character of its views when it tried, often successfully, to establish political attitude as the criterion of payment for members of people's communes. This was a kind of "material incentive" to take a political position. A political position, however, can be revolutionary only if it derives from class reasons and not from personal interest. The general application of this practice would have "resulted in the gradual transformation of the advanced political and ideological views of a vanguard into growing privileges for a minority," and in the "encouragement of political opportunists . . . always spouting 'the correct line' . . . this could easily lead to the gradual substitution of ostentatious conduct for collectivist attitudes, for a political attitude must be noticeable before it can be praised and *remunerated*. Hence, the obvious risk that the external manifestations of the revolutionary spirit will assume increasing importance."[11]

---

11. Claudie Broyelle, *La Moitié du ciel* (Paris: Denoël-Gonthier, 1973), p. 213. This book deals with problems of women and the family in China.

The bourgeois character of the ultra-left is evidenced most significantly by its de facto opposition to the appropriation by the masses of proletarian revolutionary ideology. This opposition took many forms. One consisted in dissuading the masses from serious study of Marxism-Leninism and encouraging the "study" of quotations from Mao Tse-tung "so as to get quick results."[12] This approach turns Marxism-Leninism into a set of "practical recipes" and disregards what is most essential—the assimilation of principles. It manifested itself very concretely when ultra-leftists took over the publishing field: they discontinued the publication of most of the basic works of Marxism and tried to instill in the minds of the workers the idea that Mao Tse-tung's writings (which the workers could obtain only in fragmentary form) were not part of a great theoretical tradition.

The ultra-left also manifested its opposition to the appropriation by the masses of Marxism-Leninism by replacing serious study with the stereotyped repetition of a few quotations, and even by imposing upon them the memorization of certain passages from Mao Tse-tung's writings. In 1967 it was common to see workers lined up before starting work and reciting quotations from Mao Tse-tung by heart. At the Shanghai Iron and Steel Institute, the ultra-left representative had two researchers recite the entire text of "Serve the People" in my presence. This attitude toward "study" was also shared by Lin Piao: "It is best to memorize some of his [Mao's] important passages."[13]

These ultra-leftist practices, of course, do not correspond to the valid use that can be made of the "Little Red Book." It can serve as an introduction to the study of Marxism-Leninism and Mao Tse-tung Thought provided it is not reduced to a set of practical recipes or to a series of quotations to be memorized, that is, provided it serves to prepare the

12. This expression is contained in Lin Piao's Foreword to *Quotations from Chairman Mao Tse-tung*, 2nd ed. (Peking: Foreign Languages Press, 1966).

13. Ibid.

workers for the study of Marxism-Leninism and not to divert them from this purpose. In practice, however, the ultra-left did its utmost to dissuade the masses from the study of Marxism-Leninism, particularly (and this is only apparently paradoxical) by proclaiming "the absolute authority of Mao Tse-tung Thought." They could thus say that Chairman Mao's instructions must be carried out regardless of whether or not their full significance was understood.

The ultra-left diverted the workers from serious study by enjoining them to obey mindlessly. This was contrary to what Mao Tse-tung himself had said: "Communists must always go into the whys and wherefores of anything . . . on no account should they follow blindly and encourage slavishness." Here too, the ultra-left merely adopted the substance of Liu Shao-chi's line, which also advocated "blind discipline," although in a different guise. Similarly, the cult of personality fostered by the ultra-left tended to undermine the people's confidence in Chairman Mao and encourage blind obedience to any directive allegedly emanating from him. This approach would in the long run have led to extensive manipulation of the masses.

Ultra-leftist opposition to the appropriation by the workers of Marxism-Leninism was evident in the following statement: "Mao Tse-tung's thought is Marxism-Leninism at a higher level of development. In our era, the study of Mao Tse-tung's thought is the best way to study Marxism-Leninism."[14] This was tantamount to saying that the study of Marxism-Leninism was an obsolete and unnecessary task and that it was pointless to engage in serious study of historical materialism, dialectical materialism, and the basic works of Marxism-Leninism.

Since the political defeat of the ultra-left, the basic works of Marxism and Leninism are again being widely disseminated; what is equally important, mass study of these

14. *Peking Review*, no. 46 (November 10, 1967), p. 22.

works has been strongly encouraged with a view to helping the workers "distinguish between true Marxism and false Marxism." The Chinese press is publishing an increasing number of articles by workers and cadres explaining how they are benefiting from serious study of Marxism-Leninism, and why they regard such study as necessary. The following was written by a worker-cadre:

> A worker-cadre like me has deep class sentiments for the Party and Chairman Mao as well as experience in my work, but simple class sentiments cannot replace consciousness in the struggle between the two lines and pure practical experience cannot replace Marxism-Leninism. If I should overlook the importance of studying Marxism-Leninism-Mao Tse-tung Thought, which is a summing-up of the experience of the world revolution and the Chinese revolution, I cannot avoid committing empiricist errors.
>
> Although direct experience gained from practice reflects a certain reality of the objective world, it is only perceptual knowledge and the reflection is superficial, partial and incomplete.[15]

The last sentence is aimed at another ultra-leftist tendency—to disarm the masses by one-sidedly stressing the importance of direct knowledge and advocating empiricism and spontaneism, and thus to strengthen bourgeois ideology and confuse the workers.

In consistently minimizing the importance of study and one-sidedly giving precedence to "direct knowledge," the ultra-left showed its contempt for collective experience and "forgot" that the development of knowledge requires a combination of practice and theory and the most comprehensive possible outlook. Direct knowledge is essentially partial knowledge—it is acquired in a specific place, in a specific period, by one or more individuals living under particular conditions. Granting greater importance to direct than to indirect knowledge, moreover, means substituting individual

15. "Overcoming Empiricism," *Peking Review*, no. 43 (October 27, 1972), p. 7.

practice for the national and international historic practice of the masses—a practice that must be systematized and synthesized before it can be assimilated through study. In sanctioning such a substitution, the ultra-left encouraged empiricism and tended to deprive the Chinese masses of the experience deriving from the history of national and international class struggles. When it has no access to this experience—which is summed up in the works of Marxism-Leninism and kept alive through the action of the proletarian party—the revolutionary movement is bound to regress, thus strengthening the bourgeoisie with respect to the proletariat.

Throughout the Cultural Revolution the revolutionary line combated ultra-leftist activities fostering empiricism. As these activities came under increasing attack by the revolutionary line, this bourgeois ideological tendency began to lose its impact.

There can be no question of a "definitive victory," of course; that the struggle continues is evidenced by a number of recent articles in the Chinese press, notably by the article cited earlier, "Overcoming Empiricism," which contains the following remarks:

> We would commit mistakes of empiricism if we regard direct experience as something absolute and rigid—using partial experience as an unalterable formula and applying it everywhere, using old experience to look at new things which have developed and changed, or overrating our partial experience and underrating or even denying the correct experience of others. . . . The realm of practical activity is extremely wide, but the scope of an individual's practice is always limited. While we attach importance to direct experience gained from personal practice, we should also treasure the creations of the masses, be good at making investigations and study, and learn with an open mind from other people's experience. Only thus can we do our work well. . . . One cannot have direct experience in everything. Actually most knowledge comes from indirect experience. If anyone believes only in himself and sets his personal experience against the masses' and direct experience against indirect, he will also commit empiricist

errors. . . . Because those people with empiricism neglect the
guiding role of Marxism in revolutionary practice, pay no attention to studying revolutionary theory . . . are intoxicated with
narrow, non-principled "practicalism" and with being brainless
"practical men" with no future, and lack firm and correct political orientation, they are easy ideological captives of political
swindlers who are sham Marxists.[16]

Politically, ultra-leftist spontaneism is a direct extension of
empiricism. Spontaneism asserts, as does empiricism, that
knowledge can be derived directly from a limited practice
and that the masses are therefore never in error. The Marxist
view holds that correct ideas derive from practice, and in the
first place from the practice of the masses; it is here distorted
into the notion that "all the ideas of the masses are correct."
In January 1967 *Hongqi* elaborated this ultra-leftist point of
view by advocating a life-and-death struggle and inciting the
masses to commit acts of violence against numerous cadres.
Whereas the revolutionary line warned against such practices
and advocated "struggle based on reason and facts," the ultra-
left asserted that the masses were right and could not commit
"excesses." The adherents of the revolutionary line criticized
this petty-bourgeois point of view, and warned against a
growing tendency toward "self-aggrandizement, careerism,
cliquish attitudes, individualism, and ultra-democratism," all
tendencies that were being abetted by the ultra-left.

Lin Piao, as we know, also tried to extol spontaneism. For
instance, he asserted: "The revolutionary movement of the
masses is naturally reasonable. Although there are among the
masses certain groups and individuals who commit right or
left deviations, the main current of the mass movement is
always reasonable and always conducive to social progress."
This is contrary to one of the conclusive lessons of history—
that there exist, and can exist, mass movements under bourgeois direction, as is unfortunately proven by the experience
of fascism, Hitlerism, varieties of racism, and so on.

16. Ibid., pp. 6-7.

The contradiction between the empiricism and spontaneism of the ultra-left (what could be called its assertion of "the absolute authority of the masses") and its dogmatism (expressed in its affirmation of "the absolute authority of Mao Tse-tung Thought") is an apparent one. In each instance the intended purpose is the same—to deny the necessity of studying Marxism-Leninism, to deny the role of theory and the party as indispensable instruments for helping the masses to distinguish between correct ideas and false ideas and thus to unify their activities. In each instance the ultra-leftist formulations help weaken and divide the workers. The empiricism and spontaneism of the "ultra-left" are further testimony to the bourgeois character of its political line.

The temporary and partial successes achieved by the ultra-left delayed the victory of the revolutionary line. They sowed confusion insofar as the apparent "radicalism" of the ultra-left created the false impression that it represented a genuine left current. The ambiguous character of ultra-leftist practices and assertions manifested itself at several levels.

Tactically, of course, the ultra-left did not openly proclaim itself as a specific independent current. It sought to assume the guise of an authentically Marxist-Leninist revolutionary tendency; it dissimulated its real character by interweaving its own assertions, which reveal its true class character, with Marxist-Leninist concepts and Mao Tse-tung's writings. This mixture of Marxist and revolutionary formulations and bourgeois and petty-bourgeois practices marked the real class character of the ultra-left and enabled it to deceive some workers and infiltrate the organs of power.

There is no doubt that the strictly ultra-leftist slogans quite often met with a favorable response among the laboring masses. During the transition period, in fact, the aspirations of the workers may have a twofold character. Insofar as they continue to be marked by the objective division of the masses (deriving from the reproduction of bourgeois relationships, the continued existence of capitalist factors, etc.), the workers retain a petty-bourgeois, individualist, and idealist character. At the same time, they also reflect a desire to transform the world; in other words, they also correspond to a revolutionary will. The ultra-left accordingly adapted its empiricism, spontaneism, and dogmatism to the petty-bourgeois aspect of mass aspirations. This elicited a response which became even more extensive when the ultra-left adopted some of the formulations of the proletarian line.

It was only after they had gained first-hand experience in the course of protracted, complex struggles and benefited from the assistance provided by the adherents of the proletarian line that workers influenced by the ultra-left learned to distinguish between two opposing sets of assertions: those the ultra-left had borrowed from the revolutionary line, without translating them into practice; and those whose "radicalism" was in no way revolutionary since they did not aim at genuine change but merely substituted "life-and-death struggles" and personal attacks for a real struggle to transform social relationships, in keeping with the authentic aspirations of the revolutionary masses.

Another factor also contributed to the temporary and limited successes of the ultra-left. The initial phase of the Cultural Revolution was marked chiefly by struggle and criticism and since the revisionist guise of the bourgeois line was then the focus of attack, the ultra-leftist position appeared to be closely associated or even identical with the revolutionary line. Even during this phase, the differences between the revolutionary and ultra-leftist lines were as profound and pervasive as at any other time (since they bear on the contradiction between bourgeoisie and proletariat), but they were temporarily relegated to a subordinate place, even though they were apparent in numerous publications and statements. A careful examination of these publications makes this quite clear.

But after the first phase of the Cultural Revolution—once the revisionist line had suffered major defeats and new relationships had to be developed—the bourgeois character of the ultra-leftist line (which fostered the old relationships) compelled it to abandon its apparent affinity with the revolutionary line. The struggle between the proletarian and bourgeois lines then turned into an increasingly explicit struggle between a revolutionary line and an ultra-leftist line.

During the initial phase of the Cultural Revolution the ultra-left had acquired a mass base among radicalized university and middle school students. As long as the struggle focused primarily on the superstructure—on the ideological apparatuses, universities, research institutes, etc.—the power of these radicalized youths was relatively significant. The student milieu witnessed a profuse growth of sharply contending rival ultra-leftist groups. On August 13, 1971, I had a conversation with the revolutionary committee of Peita (Peking) University, during which a young committee member characterized the activities of the ultra-left after the collapse of Liu Shao-chi's line as those of a clique which had tried to divide the revolutionary ranks: "The fact that we, young students, lacked social experience and had an undeveloped world outlook enabled these class enemies to infiltrate our ranks." He then pointed out that in June 1967 armed struggle erupted at the university, which paralyzed the Cultural Revolution. The struggles came to an end only after a workers' team arrived at the university. He added: "After we had gained this practical experience, we realized that we could not depend exclusively on the students and faculty to advance the cause of the Cultural Revolution . . . that we could not do anything without the aid of the workers and peasants."

As the focus of struggle shifted to the factories, thereby creating a vast upsurge of working-class political activity, this social base of the ultra-left became increasingly less important. When the working class finally intervened directly in the universities, middle schools, research institutes, etc., the influence of the ultra-left declined sharply. Working-class intervention led to growing mass unity around the revolutionary

line. As the ultra-left became isolated, it was driven to dissimulate its real aims and resort to personal attacks.

The proletarian line, for its part, could and had to wage a
struggle of ideas and principles. Its attacks did not focus on
individuals, except when these individuals knowingly partici-
pated in real conspiracies, but on ideas; this is why many of
those who had been deceived by ultra-leftist ideology and
subsequently recognized their errors, retained responsible
posts in the various organs of power.[17]

That the masses united around the proletarian line after a
period of confusion was due to the fact that they were able
to learn the lessons of their own experience; they were aided
in this complex task by the adherents of the revolutionary
line, by the overwhelming majority of party members, and by
their own study of Marxism-Leninism. The Chinese workers
thus gained growing insight into the deceptively "revolutionary" character of the ultra-left, into its bourgeois character. This explains why most of the former adherents of the
ultra-left were led to recognize their errors and rejoin the
revolutionary ranks. This resulted in the achievement of a
wide range of transformations in the economic base and in
the superstructure. Transformations of such scope are possible only when the workers are united around a revolutionary line.

Once the masses had achieved unity almost all the adherents of the ultra-left rallied to the revolutionary line,
frequently retaining their regular posts, and the ultra-left
literally broke up. This sudden collapse has astonished many
foreign "observers." It has also bewildered a considerable
number of political activists of various nationalities who had
been influenced by the pseudo-radicalism of the Chinese
ultra-left. Having generally followed events from afar and
having paid insufficient attention to the ideological class
struggle that was openly waged in the Chinese press for years,

17. Concerning this point see *Vento dell'Est,* no. 26, pp. 26-27.

they found it, and still find it, difficult to understand that the ultra-left, which they confused with the revolutionary line and which played such a prominent role in Chinese political life, should have collapsed so suddenly. The explanation, however, is quite simple—as soon as the Chinese workers had grasped its true class character, the ultra-left was bound to lose its mass base.

The political collapse of the ultra-left certainly had serious consequences for those of its adherents who refused to admit their errors and tried to engage in conspiratorial activities, but historically these consequences—which were seized upon exclusively by the "serious" (bourgeois) press—are but the secondary effects of the disintegration of ultra-leftist influence.

Nevertheless, the ultra-left, as we have already indicated, did not suffer a "definitive and total" defeat. The proletarian line will inevitably continue to be faced with a bourgeois line whose revisionist and ultra-leftist manifestations may well assume new guises. Such confrontations are the inescapable outcome of a class struggle which during the transition period is rooted in the continued existence of bourgeois relationships; these in turn can be eradicated and superseded by new relationships only in the course of successive revolutionary struggles. This is why other cultural revolutions will be required to continue the task initiated by the first one.

As I have indicated earlier, some familiarity with the main features of the struggle between the two lines, and particularly the struggle between the proletarian line and the bourgeois line under its ultra-leftist guise, is indispensable for an understanding of the most recent phase of the Cultural Revolution, and especially of the ideological and political conditions under which the social transformations effected by the Cultural Revolution could be realized. Although the class struggle which has been unfolding in China since 1966 is not yet understood in all its aspects and will have to be fully evaluated by the Chinese themselves, the conclusions pre-

sented here are readily verifiable through a careful examination of material published in China (and available in trans-
lation) since the beginning of the Cultural Revolution. It is
also possible that the Chinese Communist Party has made a
more extensive evaluation than would appear from published
material, for many of the discussions that have taken place in
China and the conclusions drawn from them are not necessarily made accessible in publications destined for foreign
dissemination. Furthermore, insofar as the overwhelming
majority of former ultra-leftists had made honest mistakes
and have since recognized their errors, the ideological struggle
against this line assumes specific forms. Judging by available
information, this struggle appears to be characterized by the
predominance of critical analysis of some of the *ideological
themes* of the ultra-left, and not by a systematic, overall
critique of the ultra-left as such. If such is indeed the case,
this is undoubtedly due to the fact that the ultra-left never
represented itself as a unified current, since it was itself
divided into factions and more or less contradictory tendencies, and that an ideological struggle waged in this manner
offers the greatest possibility for preserving the unity of both
the party and the masses, this being a constant concern for
the Chinese Communist Party.